Women Celebrate

The Gift in Every Moment

Stories of Adversity and Grace, Joy and Strength

Compiled and Edited
by Elizabeth Welles

A Peace Communications Book

Published by Peace Communications,
1129 Maricopa Highway #200, Ojai, CA 93023
www.PeaceCommunications.net.

Library of Congress Catalog Card Number: 2003110368

ISBN 0-9743998-0-9

Printed in the United States of America

Cover and layout by Fine Line Design

To my Mother
And my Mother's Mother
And all who have come before

To my Children
And my Children's Children
And all who will come after

To the Earth
Great, Round, Wondrous Body that you are

And to Daniel and Cathy
And the Infinite Spirit that Ignites Our Hearts

A PERSONAL FORWARD

n the spring of 1994 I put out the call for people to write for
Women Celebrate by placing ads in *Poets and Writers* and one
other writer's journal. Unbeknownst to me, the ad was lifted
and placed in several different magazines. The response was
overwhelming. A single note sounded and it struck a chord
from North America to Europe to Asia and Australia. I received
submissions from men and women from all walks of life, from
prisoners to professionals. I naively thought, three months and
I'll wrap it up by Christmas. Little did I know that it would be three months plus an
almost additional ten years before this book would find its way to the public. Putting
it together became an exercise in the practice of radical trust and patience. I was like
the person who says, "Oh, the ocean? No problem." Then in the middle of the ocean
with my rowboat and one oar, I scratch my head and say, "How did I get here?" But
you're there and so you keep on rowing. Since we know everything we need to know
when we need to know it, I had to trust that every detail would be taken care of at
the right time. It has. Through the trials, tribulations, and supreme test of the hero-
ine's journey, *Women Celebrate* has proven that, indeed, works have a life of their
own regardless of their creator's thoughts and desires. Sometimes I contemplated taking the manuscript and tossing it to the ocean, except that it always returned on the
very first wave. When I asked an advisor about putting it to bed, he said No, because
it hadn't fallen to sleep.

So what gets one through a project of such length? Pure perseverance in one's own
vision—yes, enough belief to lay all one's resources on the line with no guarantee of
results—yes, and all the people who nourished the spirit of this book by the small
gifts, letters, pictures and cards they sent through the mail that continually anchored
me to this project and impelled its movement forward.

ACKNOWLEDGMENTS

hank you to the women and men who sent forth their pieces. Whether the writer's work appears in this collection or not, their cover letters told me the words sent out to invite submissions were like a "nuclear device going off" where at last words could find shape and stories pour forth into completion. I received letters that said the guidelines gave them the impetus to put their pen to paper and write the words that had swirled in their heads and never been expressed. Letters told of "nervous break-throughs," or that writing was an "action against silence," and time to get on with their healing, and the business of living. My only regret is that I could not include them all.

Thank you to those who guide me to look within for answers and Truth.

Thank you to friends and family who offered their gifts of wisdom and insights, and to the Muse for the rare and exquisite inspiration that surrounds and blesses the continuing collaboration of hearts and minds.

Thank you to the Spirit that works through us, the Supreme Creator, by whatever name we call it. To the Great Silence within all, I am grateful.

Deepest of gratitude I extend to my parents, Daniel and Cathy Shapiro. On March 29th 1996, my father breathed the breath of Spirit when he passed from his earthly frame. I was with him months before helping him and the family. He lived his life, not speaking a harsh or negative word about anyone. He was a true peacemaker with a great joie de vivre. We loved each other with an open hand, respecting each other's journey, enjoying each other's presence. It is the greatest personal loss I experienced, and yet the unconditional love he gave not only to me but to all he met along the way, the acceptance he extended towards other's lifestyles and opinions, and the strengths he embodied here on earth, continues to flow even now, harmonizing my being and that of my family. I have always felt it is only our bodies that die at death and that our souls and spirits live and, in fact, our relationship with those that leave continues. Truly we meet again and again, and death does not exist. It is rather a transformative surge into a new and different form. He never saw with earthly eyes the completion of this book. But he knew it would be completed, published, and that it would be the first of many to come. He knows it even now. With the deepest of gratitude, it is to him I dedicate *Women Celebrate*, to him and my mother. Their unwavering love and support, confidence and strength stand by and watch its creation and birth. Their love has been with me through the creation of this work and through all of my life. It extends beyond the bounds of this world, and my love extends back to them forever and always.

These stories are offered with love.

Elizabeth Welles

TABLE OF CONTENTS

Preface and Introduction by Elizabeth Welles

CHAPTER ONE
Coming of Age – The Gift of Self

CHAPTER TWO
Gift of Our Relations – People and Places

CHAPTER THREE
The Gifts of Traveling Through Time

CHAPTER FOUR
Gifts of the Body-Lands – The Instinct to Trust the Gut

CHAPTER FIVE
Gifts of Adversity – Grief and Grace

CHAPTER SIX
Gifts From the Earth

CHAPTER SEVEN
Gifts of the Children

PREFACE

lthough this book was born of Soul, the first inkling of it appeared in June 1985, when my time with a spiritual teacher abruptly ended. I had met this teacher at the age of sixteen and stayed with him for twelve years. During these years, if I felt sad or disturbed, more than once, the Swami would say, "Oh you shouldn't feel that way," a sentiment echoed by others during my formative years. But I did feel things, differently from others. And so, I thought, I had no right to the way I felt, and therefore something must be wrong with me. Feelings got stuffed deeper and deeper, lodged further in the psyche, deeper in the body. But they never went away.

When it was revealed to the community as a whole that this teacher preached celibacy but practiced otherwise, the ashram where he resided fell apart. I began a journey to recollect the lost pieces of self and looked for another retreat. But the gentle voice of intuition whispered that it wasn't a retreat I really wanted, rather I wanted to go to the woods and live on the land. I was not turned off to spiritual study, but how that study ensued would now be different. Ultimately, the fall of the ashram was my initiation and re-introduction into women's mysteries, which reconnected me to my love and reverence for the Earth. I found a group of women going on a vision quest, and I rediscovered new roots as I slept outside on the earth for nine days and nights.

In the years that followed, the small or large shadow creatures were invited out of the closet into the open so that their pain and separation could begin to be released. I dared myself to look at patterns that caused me harm, and to break silences, to bring my vulnerabilities up to the surface not to be hurt, but to be loved—*by me,* and I found compassion for the past without self-recrimination.

I lived in the great unknown, whether I honored that unknown as a kind of grace, a water ride with cool, wet moist drops sprinkling on my skin and wind blowing on my face, or whether I honored that unknown as a kind of terror or a big gray monster that would gobble me up at any time. And I was put back in touch with the intuitive voice where I could begin to engender a real sense of self-acceptance.

I re-grew to see that the senses were the signs I could trust. But the way in which they spoke was as varied and subtle as the blades of grass. Their rhythms and tone would change, sometimes speaking loudly, sometimes in a faint whisper, but almost always through the body: the gnawing in the pit of a stomach, the melody in a heart, the tightness of a clenched jaw, the fluidity or hesitation in one's voice, a passing thought, a vision, a dream, a hunch, gut feelings, an awareness, an intuition or instinct, or just plain common sense. Sometimes the knowingness would come in a reflection of something "outside" of myself as in a bird's flight, a deer's crossing, a raccoon, a fox, the rain, or a storm. Whatever the "mystical" co-incidences, the "strange" synchronicities or co-occurrences, I found they were not so mystical or strange. They were as natural to my world as is breath or the rising sun. This sacred way of knowing, gardened and grown by life experience, sprinkled with wisdom, became a part of the grace that enfolds my life.

The years with this teacher heralded the final notes of a song played for a long time, a song I could now say *No More* to. I forgave the teacher instantly, and then years later discovered I was still angry. As soon as I recognized the anger, it easily and quickly dissolved. I remember the good times, the laughter, and yes the love. Most of all I am grateful to the experience that in some sense provided me with the lesson that cracked open the shell so I could gather more than I would have if I had continued being the "disciple." But I am not forgetful of the events that contributed to shaping my life. To forget them entirely would be to dishonor myself, all that occurred, and all that I'd learned. Rather I let the experiences inform my living now.

This experience was one of many seeds that gave forth to this book, a seed familiar enough to others as well. I met women who knew what it was to live in silence, and in fear, to be invisible in their own lives, and the world: women who questioned their instincts and intuitions, well-tuned but often neglected. I also met women who had embraced and re-discovered the freedom inherently ours even from the moment before we exploded forth into form. I wanted to provide a place, a forum for them to write about the gifts they found hidden in uncommon corners, the body of life's wondrous and vast experiences found through the senses, in whatever way sense spoke to them.

Thus begins The Gift in Every Moment.

INTRODUCTION

omen Celebrate is a compilation of stories and poems by women, celebrating the Creative impulse moving through their bodies, hearts, minds, and souls. It honors the vast array of experiences we journey through in recovering and reclaiming our joy. The journey is seeded in a deep trust and integration of the whole. It is about being present to seeing what exists in any one moment, be the experience one of challenge or delight, hardship or renewal. It is a seeing wherein tremendous power effortlessly avails itself to transform experience into a joy that is actively attentive, aware and receptive. Even in what is perceived as adversity, often a place of no answers, maps or resolution, there is wisdom, and sometimes delight. For it is in those moments that additional time is taken to listen to the feelings and forces held by the body. It is at those moments when we feel our back against the wall that we often find listening is the only thing to do.

It is a *kind* listening that opens the way for a deep inner surrender. Not a surrender of laying down to sleep, but a surrender that awakens us to embrace what is, without having to change it. Paradox becomes a source of renewal, and we are able to honor individual process, just as a sculptor honors the chip of the chisel even though the figure has yet to fully emerge. For there is Presence in the tapping, the sound of the pick against stone, just as there is Presence and Grace found in trusting our Selves and in trusting the Great Unknown. It may look like a place of confusion or chaos. Often it is the chaos out of which the figure appears, out of which quietude of Soul is born. For within experience lie seeds for discovery, compost for creativity, and treasures that creates a resilient sense of wonder to fortify us through our lives. Just as in these stories lie the twinkling knowing that says, "I am cracking open the hidden places in my life. I am breaking open the shell to stretch my legs. Like the baby's first breath, be it gentle or hard, it is life, it is the stuff of which we are made. I have lived and continue to live fully to the best of my ability."

However this does not mean that we push or pull ourselves—or anyone else—to where we, or they, are not. And it does not mean we celebrate the harrowing or difficult, for both these would be the ultimate in presumption and disempowerment. Rather we recognize the multi-dimensional aspects of Self, and the many faceted ways in which *one single* diamond lights. Respecting personal time frame and the ability to simply sit with the uncomfortable, sensing deeply into what ails, we reawaken gentleness that allows life to be lived with a vibrancy that heals ills and soothes wounds, to find ease on the other side, or right within, the dis-ease itself. Then, without having *done* much of anything at all, the energy and life force trapped in hiding, ignoring, or running from what exists is released to generously guide the ship of our lives towards more brilliant and creative shores.

Such listening is a revolutionary act supportive of innate wisdom. The world cries for this kind of listening and Self-trust—when the sun of *one's own* eyes and Truth smiles upon the shadow. But world-tears have lain on fallow and arid land because women and men too often do not recognize and go after what they want, refusing to follow, be a disciple to, or simply know what Joseph Campbell so eloquently referred to as "Bliss." Instead we chop down forests, pollute the seas and our own bodies, thinking we can own a piece of land, and conquer the Earth, when we have not seen our very Selves.

The Gift in Every Moment is not to be confused with some fleeting concept of happiness "out there." It is not a goal and therefore something to be attained. For to make it that, would be to miss the opportunity for joy along the way. Can you imagine admonishing the seed in the earth for not breaking ground and sprouting sooner? Rather we honor the journey, which at times includes ecstasy as much as terror. Tears roll down the face and there is healing in the heart. Laughter reigns and it is a hearty sound rooted in the soil of soul. The journey is sensorial and deeply felt, for joy resides in all the colors of the rainbow. If Joy had a voice it might playfully query: Can I, with all my foibles and frailties find joy in my life right now? We want to be able to answer "Yes." In that yes we find wholeness and acceptance. Our actions can then become gifts shared at a great party where we recognize what lies hidden in all people so that we can greet each other with a smile that says, "Yes, I know you. Yes, I see you. I recognize your joy and your sorrow. Come let us walk, talk, dance, and play."

Even in a world bristling with chaos, we can move and dance not from a clouded rage or wishful revenge, but from an uncompromising clarity that offers strength and persistence to keep on keeping on until the child is soothed, violence is stopped, war is halted, and the trees are left to grow.

Although I received beautiful, eloquent stories and poetry from men, I initially invited women to write for this book. I see why even more clearly now. Shortly after September 11, 2001, a date that is emblazoned on our consciences, I received an email that quoted an old Indian Proverb. "A nation is not lost as long as the women's hearts are still high. Only when the women's hearts are on the ground – then all is finished, and the nation dies. The women are the life carriers." It is time, it has always been time, but it is now time more than ever for women to come forth with our wisdom and knowledge, and our right to entitlement intact; entitlement that is not at the expense of another, but entitlement that lifts our Selves and all others up. A Norwegian proverb states, "In every woman there is a Queen. Speak to the Queen and the Queen will answer." Such Self-recognition is the gift. For we are the salt of the earth and the givers of life, whether we make babies, food, art, whether we run businesses or corporate America. We receive seed and we then give forth. We fold in and then burst in bloom. We create and we destroy. What a capacity we have to reclaim and own the beauty, strength and compassion that is naturally ours, and that we have come here, in the flesh, to celebrate. Our hearts may be bleeding and open, but they are not broken nor will not be trampled on the ground. The human heart is the largest container in the Universe, a well without end, able to hold all suffering and grief, beauty, laughter, and relief. We are strong in our vulnerabilities, unshakable in our collective resolve, and this landscape for celebration and honor of life is available not only to women, but to all people everywhere, right now. It is a landscape to be embraced as real in our hearts, for it already is.

CHAPTER ONE

COMING OF AGE
THE GIFT OF SELF

*It's all a gift wrapped
in what one may sometimes think of
as difficult packaging,
but once opened... what is longed for comes.*

*It comes from a deep inner surrender
and a deep inner knowing of who you are.*

*Inside is a gift,
a beautiful gift –*

It is the Gift of Self.

FINDING A VOICE
(THE NEIGHBORS MIGHT HEAR)

Edith A. Cheitman

y mother was not allowed to sing to my brother and me when we were children. She and my father (an amateur tenor with operatic ambitions) had agreed that exposure to her sweet, slightly off-key singing voice might interfere with our optimal vocal development. Ownership of voice in the family had been assigned to my father with my mother the smiling audience to his pronouncements, made in what I thought of as his "special" voice—resonant, pitched considerably lower than his regular voice and directed to carry from one end of our third-floor walkup apartment to the other without being heard by the neighbors.

To not be heard by the neighbors was the prime directive in our family. As time passed and my mother's despair exceeded the self-imposed limits of well-modulated silence, she reached deep within and found a loud, desperate voice to express herself to my father "later, after the children are asleep." Lying there in the dark of our shared bedroom my brother and I listened to the crescendos of our mother's incomprehensible lament punctuated by our father's familiar injunction, "Lower your voice, Therese. The neighbors will hear you."

A quarter of a century later when feminists were accused of being strident, it was my mother's nightvoice I remembered. Of course we were strident. One tends to be strident when trying to save her life.

My early exposure to womanvoice—other than the opera my father listened to in his bedroom at the far end of the long hall in our apartment—was in the clandestine hours spent with my Irish grandmother at her house. Not giving a damn about what "Himself," as she called my father, said regarding musical education, she warbled cheerily about her kitchen singing me all my favorite songs loudly and completely out of tune-like a big old honky-tonk piano. Once in a while, made bold by Granny's bravery, my mother and I joined in making a thoroughly joyful noise there in her kitchen until it was time to return to voice prison.

There was hope in the family that, with a father so musically gifted, one of his children would be, too. As eldest I was first to test the hypothesis by taking piano lessons-a seemingly reasonable enterprise since I had been picking out the tunes in my head on our big piano for as long as I had been able to sit on the piano bench and reach the keys. Somewhere around lesson six my piano teacher decided that my voice lacked sufficient range; that it was, in fact, too *deep*. Piano practice that week was thirty minutes of a one-finger exercise running up the scale as I sang "Johnny's Song Is Just One Note," presumably to upgrade my vocal range. I did not know then and I do not know now what my voice had to do with playing the piano but I was clear that I had no interest in playing or singing Johnny's damn song if I couldn't play or sing my own. An ordinarily obedient child, I flatly refused to go back to piano lessons and I never touched the piano again although the music still played—fainter and less frequently—inside my head.

In a last attempt at musical voice I answered an "emergency" call for chorus tryouts in high school. Without looking up from his keyboard the director waved me toward him, listened to me sing two notes, and waved me away, discarded. In retrospect I know that he was a very tired man at the end of a long frustrating day in a similar career with little understanding that terrified children don't vocalize well on command. Nonetheless as I left that room I felt my throat close, not to open again for forty years.

Abandoning music but not yet ready to give up the thought of having a voice, I turned to acting. I was terrific. I loved it; I wanted to do it forever. After downing half a can of malt liquor (my limit) at high school parties I could be counted on to declaim Shakespeare to an ever dwindling audience of my peers or to the trees. I didn't care about attendance; in those giddy moments I had voice.

Encouraged to study in college something that would more certainly lead to employment—obviously not acting—I turned to voice on paper. I wrote plays, essays, poems, short stories, on and on, thinking I'd solved the puzzle. Woman could have voice of a sort so long as it was not spoken. (As poet laureate of our graduating class I suffered a panic attack when it was time to read the class ode to my peers.)

I graduated from college effectively mute to authentic voice. I could speak someone else's words. I could write from my own spirit. But I would not, could not—on what felt like pain of death—speak my truth aloud.

Fortunately fate, chance, the karma lords and/or my obdurate resistance to learning to type the words of others at an acceptable speed rendered me unemployable in any field remotely related to my education and training. Typewriter in hock to the landlady of my furnished room, I found work as a door-to-door encyclopedia salesperson and began the long slow reclamation of my voice. The venue wasn't what I might wish and the ambiance left a great deal to be desired but I was engaged six days a week in vocal isometrics. It was a simple program. As a salesperson on straight commission I could talk or starve. So I talked. I persuaded, exhorted, enchanted, mystified absolute strangers. Neighbors heard me! Within an hour of my appearance at their doors absolute strangers, transfixed by the power of my voice, bought twenty-four volumes of reference materials (complete with bookcase in their choice of light or dark finish). *Mirabile dictu!*

Late at night at my favorite piano bars, after two or three stingers (my limit), I'd sing.

Barbra, Sarah, Ella, Billie. Sometimes people would listen and sometimes they wouldn't but I didn't care because I had voice again those nights. Maybe you heard me.

As time will, time passed. Things got better sometimes; sometimes things got worse; but I always made my living with my voice; by the power of *logos*. I sold, I taught, I prophesied, I therapized. Once, because when I was frightened the thing I still knew how to do best was lower my voice, I was raped because I couldn't scream for help—the neighbors might hear.

Successful at most of what I did with my voice, I was still ashamed of it—like a good sculptor apologizing for the appearance and quality of her chisel. Sometimes late at night after four or five double scotches (my limit), talking with other women, a larger, darker truth emerged: *we all hated* (the word most often used) *our voices*. We all admitted to being silenced to some extent by fear of the public exposure of the essential repulsiveness of our voices, like dreams of being naked at the airport. Somewhere out there was a vocal "10" and none of us were it. I turned away from that shared truth quickly. While I could accept the silencing of my own voice, the possibility that all women might have been rendered effectively speechless was too terrible to consider.

Two summers ago I found myself alone in an eleven room house on sixty acres of swampland in rural Maine with the nearest neighbors a quarter of a mile away. Stubborn as I am, I decided to make one more attempt to reclaim my voice. In the summer dark (so no one would see me) on the side of the house away from the neighbors (so no one would hear me) I sat and I sang again, night after night, to my favorite audience—trees. I sang Barbra. I sang Sarah. I sang Ella. I sang Billie. And after two months, one dark night I sang Edith.

Made brave by four diet colas (my limit) I taped my performance and, playing it back, I heard me making a truly joyful noise for the first time since I was in my Granny's kitchen. It wasn't a voice for Carnegie Hall and surely nothing my father would have listened to but it was a good voice, a clear voice, a voice with its own range and truth. My voice.

I cried until the sun came up for all the years I was stricken mute. By morning I was crying for joy to have my voice again.

I still make my living as a therapist with that same voice but now without apology. Recently when I was considering taking office space with another therapist, one of my clients asked, clearly concerned, "Does she *know* about you?"

Know *what*?"

"Well, about how you laugh. *You* know." My client lowered her voice conspiratorially. "Sometimes when I'm in the waiting room I can hear you and you're *laughing*."

I laughed. I roared. In my big wonderful raucous voice I laughed until the tears ran down my face. I hope the neighbors heard and I hope you are laughing, too—or screaming or crying or cussing folks out—just as loud as you can in your wonderful voice.

AH, SWEET MYSTERY

Mary Murphy

When I was a freshman in high school, I joined the glee club. That year Sister Jerome decided we should perform scenes from Victor Herbert's famous operetta *Naughty Marietta* at our Christmas concert.

None of us had ever heard of *Naughty Marietta* or Victor Herbert, but when we found out it meant we could wear ball gowns and dance with boys, we were all for it.

The boys were to wear Royal Canadian Mountie uniforms rented from a local costume company. We girls got to spend one whole morning in the big closet off the assembly room trying on fancy dresses of all styles and eras left over from former musical productions. Once we got past the intense smell of mothballs that greeted us when Sister Jerome unlocked the closet, we had a fantastic time choosing gowns, trying them on and (just so we wouldn't get sent back to class too soon) choosing other gowns and trying them on. Sister Jerome's only requirements were that the gowns be suitable for a fancy ball and that they fit.

Not a person who likes to dress up, I had a terrible time picturing myself in anything I saw. Finally after row upon row of pink satin, ivory lace, white chiffon and gold spangles, I found my dress. I think I fell in love with it because it reminded me of one my mother wore in a formal photograph in a frame on our piano.

It was mauve with off-the-shoulder long sleeves, a stiff bodice and full skirt with layers of petticoat. When I put it on I looked so unlike my usual tomboy self that kids stopped looking at themselves in the long mirror by the entrance and stared at my transformation. I didn't think of myself as beautiful or glamorous, but while I wore that dress, I looked in the mirror at someone who moved and smiled like a high school girl—someone who would go to parties and dance with boys and not be a kid anymore. Everything seemed possible in that dress.

I couldn't wait to get it okayed by Sister Jerome and added to the costume rack with my name on it. However Sister Jerome's friend Louise, who acted as costume mistress, pointed out an obvious problem with my dress. It was too big: too long, too much room in the waist and I didn't begin to fill up the bodice. Louise volunteered to take in the waist and raise the hem but the bodice was stiff with a reinforced wire frame. There was no altering it. Sister Jerome told me I'd better take it off and try another, but Louise got an idea. "We'll stuff it!" she said, and went to get toilet paper from the janitor's supply room. She came back with a whole roll, pointing out that the single sheets from the girls' room dispensers wouldn't provide the desired effect.

She began unraveling long strips and stuffing them down the front of my dress. When the roll was almost gone, the bodice stood out full and rounded and everyone admitted I looked terrific—if slightly top heavy. Carolyn Smith led a chorus of "Please, Mr. Whipple, don't squeeze the alto!"

On the day of the concert, I got stuffed into my ball gown during intermission. As the curtain opened for the second half of the program the boys were already on stage in their Mountie uniforms, eagerly awaiting the arrival of their "ladies." They looked wonderful in their broad brimmed hats, black boots and bright red uniforms, marching and saluting and standing at attention.

My ballroom partner was a bass named Gomer Pound. Gomer was from Tennessee and had a southern drawl that teachers found charming and that allowed him to get away with a lot of stuff. He wore his hair in a huge blond "Afro" that made his Mountie hat pop up and sit high on his head. It was secured by bobby pins.

When Gomer saw me cross the stage toward him, he looked shocked, but I didn't care because I was busy imagining myself as a glamorous leading lady.

We had a great stage position: Front row of the chorus right next to the leading players. I think Sister Jerome put us there because Gomer threw spitballs if he got behind anybody. Sister Jerome struck the opening chords for the beautiful finale, "Ah, Sweet Mystery of Life," and we began the graceful movements and dance steps we'd practiced for weeks.

The Mountie uniforms, authentic in detail, had a leather strap running diagonally from shoulder to belt with a small buckle at about breast-bone level. On the first line of the song, "Ah, sweet mystery of life at last I've found you," the mounties pulled their ladies to them in a warm embrace. On the second line, "Ah I know at last the meaning of it all," Gomer spun me away with a flourish. I was having the time of my life until I noticed Gomer staring at my chest. I looked down and saw that some of the toilet paper had become attached to Gomer's uniform buckle and he was pulling it out as I moved away from him. Gomer obviously wasn't thinking straight (or at all) because he took hold of his end and started pulling more of it out. I had a lot of industrial-strength toilet paper in my top and Gomer just kept on pulling. I pulled back, still singing, smiling, and trying to pretend that this was what was supposed to happen.

Captain Dick and Marietta sang the next verse alone while the toilet paper taffy pull continued. When the chorus joined in on "For 'tis love and love alone the world is seeking," I threw myself into a bear hug with Gomer and managed to tear the toilet paper along one of its natural perforations. When I stepped back, Gomer had a big wad of toilet paper in his hand and there was little between me and my dress but fresh air.

Gomer, looking dazed as usual, just stood holding the toilet paper up like he'd won it in a contest, so I hugged him again and whispered, "That was in my bra, you idiot! Give it back!" And he did. I think it was the word *bra* that activated him because on the next line, which happened to be "Ah, at last I know the secret of it all!" he grabbed my bodice frame and stuffed the toilet paper, all three million yards of it, back into my dress.

You couldn't hear the end of the song for all the laughter from the audience. Some of the parents sounded like they were screaming. I was totally humiliated and ran backstage where the kids started buzzing around us trying to find out what happened. When I saw Sister Jerome bearing down on us, I just couldn't face her and I ran up to the assembly room closet to hide, feeling very sorry for myself.

A few minutes later, Sister Jerome came upstairs, sat next to me, and started talking quietly about when she was a little girl and her mother took her to Loew's Theater in Syracuse to see the opening night of the first production of *Naughty Marietta*. It was a grand event with people dressed in furs arriving in limousines and taxis. Victor Herbert himself was rumored to be in the audience. Sister Jerome got to go because her Aunt Emma was a professional singer who came up from New York City to perform in the chorus. She danced with her mountie and sang "Ah, Sweet Mystery of Life" the very first time it was performed on-stage. Afterward Sister Jerome's mother took her backstage where Emma, still in her beautiful gown, kissed her and took her to the star dressing room to meet Naughty Marietta herself. The actress was reclining on a sofa and the room reeked of lilacs.

Sister Jerome and I were silent as she remembered and I imagined the scene. Then she thanked me for making our performance of *Naughty Marietta* almost as memorable as the first. She also told me the next time we'd try knee socks, and she went downstairs.

Until that moment in the closet, Sister Jerome never told any of us kids anything about her personal life. I guess she did it to take my mind off my misery.

I went to the mirror, straightened my dress and smoothed my home-permed hair. I looked at myself a long time, and then went downstairs to meet my mother.

INSIDE-OUT

Linda Ashear

I am an inside-out person,
tired of living under wraps,
daring only now and then
to show my not-so-silver lining.

I'm sick of living right-side out.
Now seams show. Threads hang.
I wear my size & care directions on my back:
Wash separately, gentle cycle, tumble-dry.
To prevent wrinkles, remove from dryer
immediately, or press with a warm iron.

I face you inside-out,
wear myself close to my skin.
What talent!
I have learned to be reversible.
My second nature, after all this time,
comes first.

TALK LESS

Janell Moon

I always thought when I reached fifty
I'd assist the image of aging
youthful looking and pretty I'd be
assumed I'd stay thin, have energy
because I was interested
in the world about me.

Now that I'm fifty
there are better things I want.

First of all, I'm not ashamed to be myself
and with estrogen and eating, I'm round.
My breasts, large as if full of milk.
My face has lines
it can look as if I haven't
had enough sleep, but really
I sleep all I can.

I like feeling rested
then taking a good long walk.
There are trails I like
my favorite is park land with cows grazing.
I have to watch my right ankle
recurring twist injury the doctor calls it.

I'm less interested in the world about me
than once I was
although I still call
the White House on important issues
crusade more with a pen than a foot.
I'm a feminist
but don't argue my way anymore.
My voice is deeper and I live more sure.
I feel appropriately old enough
to have all the opinions I have
now that I have a word to say
about everything
I talk less.

ODE TO JOE

Elizabeth Welles

swim at a friend's apartment building several times a week where Joe, the doorman, stands. He is always there with a ready smile and an encouraging word. If it's raining he'll say, "Don't get wet cause sugar melts," or "Did you eat too much turkey? Good, I wouldn't want you to lose that nice figure of yours." He is a clear barometer of what I feel. If I look upset, he'll politely inquire, "You look a little peaked today," and even if I am, I'll assure him I'm okay.

Joe also takes my hand and kisses it whenever I come or go. At one time he may even have asked if I minded—and I'm sure I said No, that it was okay. But then I began to change. Although his hand kissing-me chivalry was nothing more than a friendly gesture, it became an obligation I begrudgingly felt I had to fulfill. My sour-puss face upon approaching the door often had more to do with the fact that I knew he'd take my hand. If he was busy with someone else I secretly thought, "Good, I can slip by today." Yet I was unwilling to say anything to Joe for the longest time. How do you break an old habit of a friend who cares? Would I hurt his feelings? Another lost voice cried, "What about me?"

Long ago, an older, trusted spiritual teacher much abused his role by taking kisses and touching. At that time, my sense of self was too small to know that I could say "No" to that man. Here was a totally different situation. Joe wasn't abusing anything, but by my not saying what I wanted, I only hurt myself. In my heart of hearts, I didn't think Joe would want that.

So after agonizing over my swim-date coming and goings for several weeks, I decided action must be taken no matter how difficult or uncomfortable I felt. If the world spins around relationships, then it was important for me to engage in my turn—standing up. Here was a situation with which to practice without the stakes being so high. After all Joe was my friend's doorman, not my lover or child, my parent or best friend.

So after our Thanksgiving hellos, how are you and how was your turkey, Joe gave me a kiss on *both cheeks*. "Dear man," I thought as I left the building, "How can I say anything today? Maybe I should just walk home and wait for another time." But I didn't. I went back to get some ATM cash and upon leaving again, gently said," I would prefer if you didn't kiss my hand every time I left the building, but rather on special occasions, holiday occasions. It just comes from background stuff, boundary things when I was a child." I later thought of a thousand ways to say it differently, better, and even that explanation seemed too much. (He hadn't even kissed my hand that day!) But this was practice, right? Besides, I had wanted to say a little something and "break" the news easily. Joe, who probably didn't want to know the details of my life, said a kind and heartfelt, "Okay."

I felt good. I had stood up for myself and said something I had wanted to say for a long time. I also felt awful. My legs were like jelly, and I second-guessed myself all the way home. Would it change our doorman-building patron relationship forever? In this harsh, cold city had I just taken away a personal pleasure from someone who cares, and from myself, even if it was for a passing moment? Would I come to miss his hand kissing touch? Would he be as friendly and still have a kind word to say when I come and go? In saying what I did when I did, did I take away from him the two kisses he had planted on my cheeks only moments before? I was filled with apology, upset, regret. Would the private agony of my saying "No," and the fantasy of his hurt feelings build till I tossed all to the wind, and acquiesced to say, "It's okay, you can kiss my hand anytime," like I did with that teacher… and so many others long ago?

Or did the jelly legs have more to do with the fact that I had, indeed, stood up. I had just said something so small but so important. The ground was more solidly placed under my feet because I had just taken something back that long ago I had given up: the right to say "No" and to set boundaries in the way other people relate to me.

I walked by my favorite city fountain. The water didn't help. The city noises were harsh. My imagination thought Joe cared as much as I did. He probably didn't. But if he did, he can know that he helped me by simply saying, "Okay." He is one of the men that open the doors through which I learn to ask for what I want. He is an ambassador of true good will: my will.

Yes, I had grown to cherish that big, warm, smiley face in the winter's city cold, and I had come to trust myself enough to say No. He opened a door into a ground on which I found new footing. He opened a door through which I passed allowing myself to simply be, and that's the best kind of doorman anywhere in the world.

LABOR OF DREAMS

Mary Diane Hausman

There are babies seething inside me
Writhing to get out
They may just rip my skin
to get free

It does hurt this constant birthing
Of things I cannot hold for long
Some die before their first cry.
It's my own fault—
I suffocate them under my tongue
Or beneath my heavy fingers that refuse
To lift pen or brush or chisel.

The ones that make it?
Well, they fear dying too,
So are persistent in their pushing,
Till at last I give up,
Ignoring their sucking mouths and
Squinting eyes and grabby little fingers
I take a deep breath,
Open my legs, and let them slip
Or pour or jump or carve
Their way out and push up my breasts,
Squeeze my nipples till the milk runs red
And I feed those hungry little souls
Till they fall asleep across my eyes,
My chest, my belly.

I lay back on the pillow of my
Efforts, gaze at my little babes
Of every color and texture across my canvas,
Every word spread across my desk
    Green and Sky
    River, Mountain and Tear
    Push and Shove,
    And slide on down into

Sweat and Bone, Pearl and
Flashy White Smile,
Poppy Blood
And Oozing Mud

Then, I think,
Yes, these are the
Ones that wanted to be,
To be here bad enough to hurt me.

And all the hair-pulling and sobbing,
All the ignoring and making-love-
Instead-of, all the going-to-pieces,
All walks for days on end and
Long drafts of a cold one,
All the sitting and staring out the window
Make no difference now.
These babies were meant to come.

These dream babies,
These brush strokes of my thighs, these
Penned wisps of my eyelids flutter.
These precise cuts of my carving tool fingers
They were meant to come.
I couldn't stop them. I tried.

It's a good thing they didn't care
What I wanted.

FREE FLOATING...
BEARING THE CROSS

B. L. Wadas

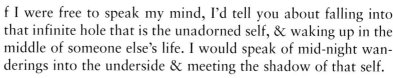f I were free to speak my mind, I'd tell you about falling into that infinite hole that is the unadorned self, & waking up in the middle of someone else's life. I would speak of mid-night wanderings into the underside & meeting the shadow of that self.

I would expound on belief in lies & and altered reality. I would tell you how it feels to understand someone else's madness, 'cause you are on speaking terms with your own.

We could compare notes on how it feels to see the feelings you mistook for love were desperation. Then you could watch yourself go blind in your mind's eye.

I'd tell you of the shock and horror of discovering that your life, your whole everyday walking-around life, was falsehood. I would discuss the confusion of finding out the things you thought were important mean nothing, not one damn thing to anyone but you. A life of contrivance, that others saw and knew all along but were too polite to mention.

I'd tell you what it's like to reside in an abyss of your own making, an abyss in which you must trust in something you are not even sure exists. An abyss in which you must give up the worship of your mind.

I would speak on the horror-terror of guilt, of being killed by guilt for doing just exactly what you thought was correct, what you were "told" was proper, what you imagined was appropriate.

Then I would tell you that the guilt is not real either, not in the way you are feeling it. I would shed light on the great lie, the lie that says: "just do the right thing, follow the rules and all will be well," only the right thing keeps changing, and your rules no longer apply.

I would tell of midnight to daylight beatings, being beaten around and around as you travel your bed at night, convicted of every sin you "in your rightness committed." I would speak of the lack of solace found in, "I just didn't know; I thought I was doing the right thing." I would speak on the need for Amazing Grace, and not knowing what that means.

If we were close—you know, best friends—we could compare notes on what it feels like to stand naked in front of God and a mirror. But hell, that conversation calls for pathological honesty, right? If we were just hanging out—you know, having fun—we could laugh about how it feels being hit up side the head with that cosmic baseball bat. Brought low and made to kneel down inside yourself, inside yourself!

I would tell you how it feels to finally see you were living a made-up life. A thing imagined by your head. Something created, designed to comfort that has turned into a mean and unmanageable fantasy. A fantasy from which the only way out is in; but first you must not only accept, you must *"embrace"* the error of your ways.

Then and only then, you will see that suffering unremitting guilt for not doing better than your ability or seeing past your level of awareness, is the ultimate form of arrogance. You will come to understand, that *never* questioning one's own rightness is the ultimate form of blasphemy. If I were free to speak my mind, I would speak on the relativity of truth and the slickness of reality.

After all that we could take a walk to the park and celebrate the wonder of breaking free. We could dance to the joy of coming into the fullness of who we really are; loose pieces, cut diamonds and all. We'd rejoice in the resurrection, yeah the resurrection.

OLIVE GIRLS

Mary Crescenzo

I am a person of color
an olive girl
a spaghetti bender
a—With-out-papers
do Wop Wop
whose ancestors
are Ellis Island immigrants

I am hot red pepper
the blood of grapes in my veins
I am cool anise on ice
and smooth Perugina chocolate
melted and hand dipped

I am every note in La Scala
every brush stroke in Da Vinci's hand,
my heart, the chestnut of peasant bread
my soul, Mt. Vesuvius on a good day

I am a Milano blonde
Sicilian redhead
the passion of Neapolitan nights
the dawn of Capri

There was a time I'd run
from the olive boys
run from their fists
run from their kitchens
run from myself
Now I stand tall as an Italian Cypress
who, on the ceiling of my chapel,
touches fingertips
with the God of my bones.

THE READER

Allegra Howard

She draws the damask drapes
sips a neat Tio Pepe
while Woolf, Wharton, and M. Sinclair
pulsate in lamplight's flush.
Alone, she eats cold chicken tarragon
watches herself
later tonight when she will
discreetly bear in her arms
those books, metronomes of her life
which have kept her
aloof from women preferring
coffee, needlework, and gossip;
bear in her arms those books,
trusting and still pulsating,
to a senior center
neoned with notices
of factory outlet field trips,
bingo Thursday nights.
There she will root them
between *Modern Maturity*
and *Retirement Now.* All her old
alternatives will appear,
and alongside them,
honed, her reasons for not choosing them.

BENEDICTUS ES DOMINE

Elisavietta Ritchie

hank You that I'm curled up here with a lover, this lover, my lover, not mine, but with me ten years (albeit for one he strayed).

Thank You that I finally strayed as well, with equal success and anguish.

Thank You that before our loving this morning, he cleaned up the kitchen after the resident mice. Thank You for returning the marmalade tom from across the soybean field so he'll tackle our mice again, and that he merely scares them back into their walls, retreat forestalling slaughter.

Thank You for swans in the cove, deer in the wood, geese overhead, and No Hunting at least on Sunday.

Thank You for propelling my daughter this way with her loaves of cinnamon bread, also that this particular morning she hasn't knocked yet. Thank You that she got through medical school and without my selling the house, and that both miraculous sons have survived their youth.

Thank You for the Hispanic lady, with pancake makeup and platinum eye shadow, escaped from several Latin dictators, and that she xeroxed our 876-page manuscript for just four cents per page and claimed she adored what she read between feeds.

Thank You that despite Your frequent absence from the macrocosm beyond, You still hover, if never enough.

Thank You for Your patience even with those of us who reject You on intellectual principle.

Thank You for letting me now again lay me down to sleep after such loving. And in fact, should You choose that I die before I awake, You'd be getting a bargain in gratitude, whereas if you wait till I'm ailing, old, alone, and quite likely daft, You'll hear symphonies of complaints. So take what You can while I'm worth the take.

· And thank You for waiting this long.

CHAPTER TWO

GIFTS OF OUR RELATIONS
PEOPLE AND PLACES

I am of Creation's colors brushed with ten thousand others.
Though we change the names, we remain the same
surrendered and still to what the painting will reveal.

We are the painted and the painters
washed away and re-emerging,
made up from so many layers of grains of sand,
one people, one home, one land.

I DON'T REMEMBER

Ruth Lehrer

When I was a little girl, my mother always countered my way of handling life's vicissitudes with her way, the "correct way." Ma was four-foot-seven, appeared seven-foot-four. Like a queen, she made her pronouncements and expected that I'd follow them without question. *My* way was relegated to oblivion. She simply forgot it.

"You will not wear those shoes," Ma declared one day, spying my dirty brown and white saddles. She trusted that I'd wear them polished and buffed "the right way," although I informed her that dirty was in, that none of the girls wore clean shoes anymore. When my trendy, grungy ones surfaced again days later, Ma told me she was "shocked." Why was I wearing those ugly shoes?

I reminded her that no one wears clean saddle shoes. "Remember our conversation?" I pleaded.

"I don't remember," she answered, reaching for the Snow White shoe polish. Ma had conveniently forgotten our disparate viewpoints. She remembered only her way, "the right way."

Crushed by Ma's disapproval of my youthful foibles, my throat constricted. I did not—could not—tell her how devastated I felt. Instead I developed headaches and stomach spasms. They worsened whenever I heard her utter those three little words, "I don't remember." This pattern of communication remained unchanged throughout the years.

Ma was "shocked" that day three years ago, the day before my sixtieth birthday, when I plucked her blue paisley from the closet, and proposed that she wear it to my party.

"Your party? Tomorrow? What party? I don't remember."

Those three little words, my heart began to pound. How could she have forgotten that interchange, which triggered in me a whopping migraine four weeks earlier? I wanted to remind my little mother, approaching her ninetieth year, of all the "better" ideas she had offered when I told her about the celebration I planned.

"Saturday night? Sunday afternoon is better."

"It's a more convenient time for everyone, Ma."

"You're not inviting your nieces and nephews? You have to invite them."

"I'm keeping the group small, just the immediate family."

"You should invite Claire. She'll be in town that week."

"Then I'll have to include all the other cousins."

"Lily's daughter doesn't like that restaurant."

"The chick peas in the salad bar are almost as good as yours."

"It's not the way to celebrate your birthday."

In the intervening weeks my enthusiasm for the party waned, but I pondered Ma's advice. Her viewpoint did, after all, have merit. I acquiesced to Ma's wishes much of the time because it was the easiest thing to do. Besides, mother was often right. Don't mothers know best?

My party? My birthday dinner? She did not remember. Stomach spasms gripped me. My throat constricted. Pain spread to my neck and swept up my jaw and down to my chest. Years of thundering silence possessed me and saturated the room. My mother did not hear the torrent of words that remained glued in my throat, as always.

Should I tell this frail old woman how distressed I become, have always become, when she disapproves of me; when she dismisses me? Won't I cause her distress? What will I accomplish? Tomorrow I celebrate my sixtieth birthday; I need to accept responsibility for my reactions. I keep the tears from surfacing and mend the hem in the blue paisley.

Thirty-five years earlier, after the birth of our first son, my husband and I left a deposit on a new cooperative garden apartment in the suburbs. We were living in a studio apartment in a six-story tenement, a short bus ride away from my parents. The landlord had offered us a larger apartment overlooking a busy concourse, but we had chosen green grass and newly planted trees.

"You'll take the apartment in your building," Ma proclaimed. "It's better here than in the suburbs. I'll baby-sit on Saturday nights. If the baby is sick, I can come and help out. When you come for dinner on Friday nights, you can take home enough food for the rest of the week. It's less expensive to commute, your husband can take the sub-way... It's better."

The day I told my mother we were moving to the garden apartment, she told me she was "shocked."

"Garden apartment? What garden apartment?" She did not recall our chat. My husband didn't take the subway the next day; he needed to stay home from work to care for our infant. I could not lift my head from the pillow.

Three years after my birthday dinner and more than three "forgotten" incidents later, I rush into my mother's senior residence and ring the bell. No one buzzes back. Can-didates for city council are speaking in the lunchroom at eleven o' clock and I am four minutes late for my appointment with Ma, who does not attend many communal functions, but has reluctantly agreed to come to this one. Concluding that she is not in her apartment, and therefore must be saving a seat for me, I envision the usual crowd in the lunchroom and my mother waving to me as my face appears in the doorway. I search the crush of familiar faces, but cannot find her. Her friend Lily gestures that she is not there, she has not seen her today.

Something is wrong. She expects me. We set this appointment up last week. She must have fainted, maybe worse—a diabetic coma. I see her on the floor, unable to get to the phone. My heart begins to race. I run from the elevator and hear the TV through the door. I fumble with the key and finally get into the apartment. My mother, in her blue paisley, is munching a fistful of chickpeas and peering at her twenty-one inch screen.

"Didn't you hear the outside bell?" I ask, trying to catch my breath.

"I wasn't sure."

"I thought you'd be waiting for me in the lunchroom."

"I'm watching my program."

"But we had an appointment to listen to the speakers!"

"I don't remember."

"You don't remember? I reminded you on Wednesday."

"You should have reminded me again yesterday."

"I go to school on Thursdays. That's the day I'm in the city all day. You know that's the only day I never have a chance to call or visit."

"So, I forgot. I'm an old lady; I forget."

"Your memory is better than mine," I hear myself blurt out. "You don't forget when Claire comes to town or what restaurants Lily's children don't like." I feel my throat tightening, my heart thumping—but this time the words do not get stuck; a torrential outburst drenches the room and my tears fall unchecked. "Every week I take classes on Thursday, and every week you phone and ask why I was not at home, and what am I studying anyhow? You don't hear me, and what I do is unimportant. That's why you forget. You've always got a better way to do it, and if I don't do it your way, you forget. I could never please you when I was growing up, and I can't please you now."

I look at my mother's face which stares back at me, wounded and uncomprehending. It does not matter. My mother is ninety-three, survivor of life's most tragic trials. Maybe—just maybe—*forgetting* is why she is still with me today, still so pretty in blue paisley. I know she will not change, will not even remember. But for me, the perpetual thunder has subsided.

I'm now able to communicate with Ma without my body parts intruding. I can look at her disapproval, even her forgetting, without feeling devastated. Ma looks at my off-off-white walking shoes and declares that they need polishing.

"Yeah, they do," I nod my head and smile.

HITCHHIKERS

Helen Frost

"I don't want nothin' stickin' to my shirt,"
Ebony told the nature guide. Hitchhiker plants,
stuck on other children's shirts like spiders,
repelled her, drew her in, until she said, "O.K.
a small one," tilted her head to see it stick.

Tired tonight, I want to sleep, don't want nothin'
stickin' to my shirt. The phone rings. Someone
I don't know I care about tells me
her mother's tumor is malignant. "Six months,"
she says, and in the pause when I can't see

what she expects of me, my cheeks get wet
throat too dry to speak. It's not
the memory of my father, though his last
"six weeks to six months" lengthened
into thirteen awful months. And it's not

the future, not my mother, or myself
I think of. I'm not translating
her life into mine. I'm saying O.K.
You're rubber. I'm glue. What you say
sticks to me. May that comfort you.

for Kate Coles

HOW TO BE A WOMAN

Deborah Shouse

or a moment the mother holds you. You are surrounded by melted mountains of her softness. You are her arms, she is your heart and you are safe and fed.

Too soon, she sets you down and straightens you up. She tugs, tucks, ties, tightens. She braids, belts, binds the reeling reckless richness of you.

You go into the bathroom while she is bathing and she covers herself with a brown washcloth and a flutter of hands. What is the mystery of the covered triangle, the tips of the breasts?

You sit on the toilet because you have to go really bad, and you see her hiding from you. You realize you should be hiding, too.

How to be a woman is its own mystery. You look at pictures of beautiful women in magazines and they are not you: they are ivory blushes and tremulous breasts of great bounty and lanky forever legs.

Your mother warns: don't let your hips speak too loudly, don't let your breasts laugh and giggle under the cotton of your shirt, don't let the butter linger long on the upper curve of your lip. So you shove aside your woman and you concentrate on men. Who are they and what do they want? How do you please these powerful animals? Does it take cleansing yourself, opening your legs and scrubbing away the scent of a wet leaf-covered forest trail, erasing the taste of child just waking up in the morning?

Your stomach longs to lounge, invites a loitering hand, meandering mouth. Your breasts sigh and lean to kiss the earth. Yet you bind them, wire them into obedience.

Your eyes see too much and run rivers.

The world is wary of your wet.

The world is wary of your wet sopping womb, so you pat yourself dry, clog yourself with cotton, act like a child isn't draining through you. You sit in meetings, poised, pointing out problems, offering solutions and you feel the flow of blood, a child escaping, an angel sliding away, a sublime possibility forever lost. You cross your legs and act like it doesn't matter.

And so, tucked and tightened, taught and tied, you leave behind your woman.

Yet she is there, keen and keening inside you, she uprises with a touch, she spreads herself for the hunger of a man. But there is so much more to her.

You rediscover her by looking into another woman's eyes. Lying next to this woman, you feel who you really are, the wonder soft invitation of your fleshy wealth, the rolling rich geography of your moist modest valleys and sloping hills. You are a river of cum and tears and spit and sweat: you are an infinite home of the heart, a swallow who never stops flying. You are a generous soul with sleeping space for everyone, a kept promise. You are a child falling into ready arms.

You look into her eyes and you see all the woman you are, all the woman you could be, all the woman you have hidden away. You cannot breathe. You cannot believe it: woman is a wealth and wisdom beyond what you dared imagine.

You look into her eyes and see the beginning bud of all you can be.

LISTEN

Francesca Garvey

or quite some time it was difficult for me to tell people I am a widow. It was easy to write it on forms—all I had to do was put a tick in a little square box with a sharp pointed pencil. Yet I found it was impossible to say the actual word. Once spoken, the sound would simply linger in some empty space, waiting to be heard. But no one ever entered that space and allowed its resonance.

And so, there was no place for the melody of that word to be played. People looked perplexed when I said you'd been dead for almost fifteen years. *You don't look like a widow,* was always their first comment. What they meant is I must have been very young when you died. I was. And what they also sometimes meant was it was hard to believe a Black woman could be a widow. It was very confusing to understand I could be more than just a single mother.

I was 24 when you died. At an age when most people are only contemplating marriage, we had been together for almost six years. Married and in love and loyal and faithful throughout the late 1970's. People found that odd also, and were fascinated by it, by you, by me, by us. The whole time we were together, there were always questions to be answered.

What's it like to be married, the feminists would ask me. *What's it like to be married to a White guy,* the Blacks would ask me. *What's it like to be married to an intellectual,* the working people would ask me. *What's it like to be married to a Catholic,* the atheists would ask me. *What's it like to be married to an Irishman,* the Americans would ask me. *What's it like to be married to the same person for so long,* the liberals would ask me.

Then, as suddenly as it started, the questions stopped. You were dead. No one asked, *What's it like to be a widow.* No one asked me anything anymore.

No longer having to answer questions silenced me. I would long for an inquiry, pray someone would say, *What's it like.* But no one ever did. I was no longer interesting. I had done something that people don't know how to talk about. I had become a widow.

I stopped talking about you because there was no one able to listen. Even God could not hear my voice. I begged Him to bring you back. I pleaded with Him to take me to you. I implored Him to give me someone to take your place. I apologized to Him for my loneliness. I hoped He would forgive me my tears. I feared He would never forgive my longings. I prayed He would listen to me.

Then one day I stopped asking Him to help me. I decided I was on my own. I turned my back on anything and everything that had been a part of you, of me, of us. Our politics. Our religion. Our Church. Our fidelity. Our humility. Our grace. Our books. Our ideas. Our determination. Our devotion. Our love. Our faith.

We had cultivated these things together. They were what kept us alive and happy. But I didn't want them anymore. I didn't want to talk about them anymore. I had no one to talk to. I was on my own. And on my own, I would find a voice. It would not be the voice of a widow, because no one could hear what a widow has to say.

I lived twelve years this way. You never existed. People would tell me how beautiful our child was and I'd nod politely. I changed her name on the birth certificate. I would not let her be a part of you because you did not exist anymore. Sometimes I just wrote Not Applicable on the forms required for school registration and things like that. I went along, on my own, and tried to forget that you ever existed.

I stopped writing. I stopped reading. I stopped going to Mass. I stopped working on political committees. I stopped reading newspapers and journals and reports. I stopped watching public television. I stopped doing all the things you and I had done together. Nothing of yours, of mine of ours, was allowed into my life.

I left the city where we had lived together. I left the people we had known together. I left the beach where we had swam and walked and made love together. I left the books and records and artwork and plays we enjoyed together. I left everything that had to do with us and went out on my own.

I was good on my own. Once in awhile something would remind me of you. But I would shove it away, throw it out, crush it before it could grow. I emptied myself, drained myself, cleansed myself of anything that had to do with you.

Yet you followed me wherever I went. Caused me to form a frown on my forehead, kept a worry in my eyes. You called to me. You searched for me. You lingered in the back of my heart and kept a constant pain churning there.

This made me very ill. I went to doctors. They told me I was severely depressed. They told me I needed therapy and medications. They told me I needed to be observed for 72 hours. They told me I needed to get over you.

I knew it was time for me to begin talking because I was being asked to explain things. I took the pills they gave me and I paid 35 dollars a week for one hour therapy sessions. They asked and I answered. They listened and I talked. They wrote and I signed forms. They decided and I agreed.

I explained you away. I told them you had been a quick affair. I had chosen to have a child with you because I was a liberated modern woman. I had not been married to you. I had not been a Catholic. I had not been a university student. I had not lived with you. I had not loved you. You, me, us—it simply never existed.

After all the questions and all the answers, the decision was made. I would move to another new city. I would get a good job. I would start all over again. I would take the pills regularly. I would rebuild my credit. I would save and buy a house. I would prepare myself for a new relationship. And I would never mention you or your name again.

I moved on. I bought a new wardrobe. I got a new hairstyle. I wore new make-up. I celebrated my thirty-sixth birthday and admired how good I looked for my age. I kept myself calm and comfortable with the pills and never mentioned you to anyone I met in my new life.

Then, one night, I saw you. I had just turned out the light and was admiring the shapes of the pine trees in the early Georgia summer ouside my window. There was no moon in the sky and the only light came from the million stars I was trying to count. I had taken my pills and wanted to sleep.

But the stars trickled through the velvet night the same way moonlight used to flow through your ebony hair.

At first, I didn't know it was you. I could not recognize you because you looked different. You were weary, tired, exhausted. Your hair was thin and limp. It hung around your haggard face in tangles. Your eyes were sunken and encircled with shadows. Your face was a lined with the creases of tears. Your mouth was drawn down at the corners and your lips trembled. Your hands shook as you held them out to me.

·I called the police. I told them there was a strange man in the woods outside my apartment. They told me to lock the windows and doors and turn on the air conditioner. I did this. The noise of the ventilation system drowned out the silence of the night. I bought a nightlight and slept with it near my bed. I kept the curtains drawn tightly.

Still, I kept seeing you. Sometimes you would be on the seat in front of me on the subway. Sometimes you would be walking past me in the grocery store. Sometimes you would be sitting at the bar of the dance club I liked. Sometimes you would be a delivery boy on the job where I worked. Sometimes you would be the bus driver. Sometimes you would be Black, other times White, other times Mexican, other times Asian.

I slept with you every time I saw you. I kissed you. I smiled at you. I went places with you. I dressed up for you. I caressed you and made love to you. But I never spoke your name.

Still, the shadows remained around your eyes. No matter what I did, you looked more ill each time I saw you. Until I began to hear you. You made the wind howl and the trees bend. You made the sky bright with lightening. You made the earth tremble with thunder. You made the ground gag on the thousands of buckets of rain you splashed down. You sent a heat wave through my apartment that blew all my electricity. My night light was shattered as you surged through it.

I saw you standing at the foot of my bed. You were a wisp of a form. I could see bones pierce your fingers as you reached toward me. The lightening flashed and I saw you heave with sobs. Your body shook and I heard your heart moan in pain. I stared, enchanted, when you began to speak.

I stayed up all that night. I didn't take you into my bed. I simply listened to you. I let you explain things to me. You told me you had been afraid. In that moment when death spoke your name, you had cried out, begged for mercy, pleaded for more time. Your eyes had searched in vain for me, for your mother, for your brother. Your ears had strained to hear our laughter, our voices, our breathing. Your hands had clutched at the formless shadows of us that tried to hold onto you. Your mouth had burned for lost smiles and kisses. You had longed to live to smell the new spring grass, the budding roses, the first summer rain.

But none of us had been any match for death. You had been taken so suddenly, so cruelly, so painfully. Your brother tried to catch up with you, in a rush of heroin and whisky. Your mother let her heart stop beating. And I froze a weak smile onto my lips, shook my hair of the dust of you, and trod like a zombie through the empty landscape of the life left to me.

And for all those years, you searched for me calling in vain. Making me run faster and faster, away from you, into places and things that frighted you as you followed me.

You told me all these things and more. How sorry you were to have left me. How my loneliness haunted you worse than you haunted me. How frightened you had been that I would gain enough distance to leave you behind forever. How much it hurt that I refused to speak your name.

Until your hands were entwined in mine and your eyes filled with tears. Until you trembled and shook and sobbed against my shoulder. Until I knew once again the warmth of your breathing across my chest, the silkiness of your hair against my cheek, the velvet of your arms around my waist. Until I was able to cry as I said your name.

I played your favorite music. I made tea for you. I encouraged you to sit on the edge of the bed so I could comb the tangles from your hair. I rubbed your sore shoulders and back as you laid against me. I smiled at you. I felt what you felt. Smelled what you smelled. Tasted what you tasted. Saw what you saw. Heard what you heard.

The next day I bought a sketch book. I began drawing you every night when you came to me. I painted you. I wrote down what you said. I listened to you some more. I filled the entire book and bought another one.

Since then, I write every day. Everything you tell me, I record it carefully. I write that I am your wife. I write that I am your friend. I write that I am your lover. I write that you have grown beautiful in the three years since you found me. I write that you are not tired and weary and sickly looking anymore. I write that you are no longer ill.

I say your name and you come. I take the hand you offer to me. It is warm and healthy and full of your pulse. I take hold of it and go wherever you take me. I journey with you through the things that keep us alive and happy. Everything that had been a part of you. A part of me. A part of us. Our politics. Our religion. Our church. Our fidelity. Our humility. Our grace. Our books. Our ideas. Our determination. Our devotion. Our love. Our faith.

No one asks me questions anymore. I answer no one anymore. There are no more questions. There are infinite answers. Edward, you are gone but not forgotten. I am your widow and will always remember you. I write this over and over again until I begin to smile. I have everything of you. Of me. Of us. I am your widow and I love you.

CHEESECAKE

Susanne Sener

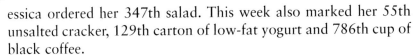essica ordered her 347th salad. This week also marked her 55th unsalted cracker, 129th carton of low-fat yogurt and 786th cup of black coffee.

Jessica knows all of this because for the past three years she's kept a food diary. Every bite, every crumb, neatly entered in the lined ledger. Including encounters with Ben and Jerry's premium ice cream, reluctantly recorded when Jessica breaks down after weeks of consuming only vegetables and diet sodas.

We're sitting in the Star Diner. Chrome countertops, gold-flecked Formica tables, neon pink vinyl booths. On the walls, posters framed in gold: Betty Grable's high heels, Jane Russell's clinging sweater, Marilyn Monroe's floating skirt.

Jessica barely touches the tines of her fork in a side dish of salad dressing. Spearing a cucumber slice, she tells me that if Betty or Jane or Marilyn were actresses today, they'd be labeled "big girls" and dismissed from the studios.

I sip from a mug of coffee, extra cream, as Jessica chews the cucumber slice. Jessica hates cucumbers but says they're a "free food," meaning she doesn't have to record them in her ledger. Raw vegetables are a guilt-free food, she tells me.

But tonight, having satisfied a craving for a thick burger and fries, I don't feel guilty. I feel quite proud. Earlier, when the teenage hostess led me to a table for six, I quietly but firmly requested a booth.

"But wouldn't you be more comfortable at a table?" she asked. Miniature teddy bears dangled from her earlobes.

"I'm having dinner with one friend tonight, not five. A booth will suit us fine."

A booth or a table, tall or queen size, department or specialty store? These are the decisions you must make when you weigh what I weigh and wear the size I wear.

Jessica's dress size is an 8. Usually. Sometimes she's a 10 or 12. That's when she's having affairs with Ben and Jerry. But sometimes she's almost a size 6. Days of salads and diet sodas. Days of headaches and nights of hunger pangs, all in the quest for this elusive perfect size.

The skin under Jessica's eyes is the color of plums. She says it's just from the fluorescent lights.

Danielle, the waitress, approaches our booth. She's uniformed in pink polyester, a smear of mustard on the edge of one pocket.

"Can I get you ladies anything else?" Danielle asks, suspending our check over the basket of artificial sweetener.

Jessica pushes away her mug of black coffee, her third tonight. "No dessert for me. I'm on a diet."

Danielle shifts her head in my direction. "And you?" I wonder if she's referring to dessert or diet.

Jessica once said that large women in restaurants should always skip dessert. It would be too revealing, like sunbathing nude in a public park. I lean my shoulders against the pink vinyl. "I'll have the cheesecake, please. With strawberry topping."

Danielle retracts our check and shoves it into the mustard-stained pocket. She leaves, then returns with a slice of cheesecake on a white plate. Sitting before me, the cheesecake is an inviting wedge crowned by glossy strawberries.

Jessica groans and leans closer to the slice. "Cream, cholesterol, butter, fat. A heart attack on a plate." She repeats her favorite mantra. "A moment on the lips, forever on the hips."

She stares at the slice, consuming it with her eyes. "I've succumbed to 24 slices of cheesecake in three years. Then hated myself the next day. They're the worst kinds of one-night stands, cheesecakes. The morning after they're gone, vanished, leaving you with nothing but an empty bakery box and a guilty stomachache."

A strawberry rolls down the side of the cheesecake. Jessica licks her lips and swallows.

I push the cheesecake toward her. "Have a bite."

It's what she's been waiting for me to say.

"I couldn't…"

I take my fork and carve out a sliver. "This bite won't count as your 25th slice. I promise."

Jessica savors the cheesecake, closing her eyes and leaning against the booth. "God, this is so good." For a second I wonder if her lover can inspire the same ecstasy as the cheesecake.

I don't know exactly when it was that I began my love affair with cheesecake. Although I do know cheesecake has always been a part of our family. Especially during celebrations, holidays, birthdays.

My sixteenth birthday my mother took me to a Broadway matinee. I felt so grownup as I sat straight in the narrow red seat, clutching the playbill in my hands. Anticipating the strike-up of the band, the raising of the curtain, the magic about to unfold.

Afterward, my mother and I huddled against the chill wind swirling down the gray tunnel that was the street. My mother fastened the top button of my coat even though I was sure I had already done so in the theater lobby. "After your grandmother and I used to see a Broadway show," she draped her plaid scarf over my collar, "we always stopped to have coffee and dessert." She slipped her leather gloved hand in my mittened one. "And talk. How does that sound to you?"

Despite the button, the scarf, and my berry-red mittens, it was then that I knew I'd reached womanhood in my family.

My mother and I bustled down the street, our heads lowered against the wind. I wondered why each time we'd pass a cubbyholed coffee shop my mother shook her head and clutched her purse closer to her side.

"Your birthday deserves a special celebration. We'll have cheesecake and coffee at Chester's on Broadway. I haven't been to Chester's in years." She gave my hand a squeeze. "You haven't lived until you've indulged in a slice of Chester's Famous Cheesecake."

Mom opened Chester's oversized menu. "It has been a few years…," she whispered, but not to me. She fumbled with the latch on her black vinyl purse. "I need to freshen my lipstick," she said, rummaging inside. I heard the clink of house keys, the rustle of tissue, then the snap, not of her lipstick case, but of her change purse. Mom spilled the contents on the table, her hands fluttering over the silver and copper.

I told my mother I wasn't really in the mood for cheesecake after all. Maybe a strawberry shake at Howard Johnson's instead.

Fifteen years later, I've still never indulged in Chester's Famous Cheesecake. If Mom were here now, would she say I've never lived?

Jessica whittles another bite of cheesecake.

"I thought everyone in your family always raved about your grandmother's recipe."

Gammie's Best Cheesecake. Three pounds of cream cheese. Two cups of sugar. Five eggs plus two egg yolks. One half cup of heavy cream. Four other ingredients, secret ingredients. All carefully combined and baked into a voluptuous blonde round.

I can see Gammie now, holding the cheesecake in her oven-mitted hands, her face misted and pink from hours in the kitchen. Hours spent preparing the holiday dinner. And the holiday desserts. Gammie would say that we'd have two dinners every holiday. First the turkey dinner. Then the dessert dinner.

So many desserts on their Lennox serving dishes, glittering like jewels on the lace tablecloth: rum cake and chiffon cake on pedestal plates with their glass covers sparkling underneath the teardrops of Gammie's chandelier, Aunt Clare's chocolate soufflé, Holly's first deep-dish apple pie, white velvet meringue piled atop my mother's lemon pie, and fudge brownies for my brothers.

And in the center of the table, on the highest pedestal of them all, the queen herself: Gammie's Best Cheesecake.

Gammie would ring the crystal bell, signaling the commencement of dessert. My mother and Aunt Clare would serve, slice after slice of pie and cake, sometimes two on one plate. No one would speak except to utter compliments between sweet mouthfuls. When Grandpa Jonathon took thirds on cheesecake, it was the men's signal to retreat to the study where they'd watch football and good-naturedly complain about the women of our family always stuffing them tighter than turkeys.

Then my mother, Aunt Clare, Holly and I would gather about the dessert table with Gammie presiding at the head, wearing her costume jewelry and homesewn clothing like she'd purchased them on Fifth Avenue. We'd pour coffee and serve each other one last slice of dessert, the slice that would see us through the next few hours. We'd talk and laugh, share secrets and stories, the meringue on my lemon pie wilting, the coffee in my cup growing cold.

Jessica stirs another package of artificial sweetener into her mug. "So many desserts. So many second helpings. Were all of the women in your family…" She pauses; she's not looking at me, "Big women?"

Armed with her flagging willpower and a battle-lined ledger, Jessica is at war with her body. The women in my family were never at war with our bodies, for we never recognized there was a conflict. Friendship and family are important to us, not calories and cholesterol.

We are big women, with big arms, big thighs, big breasts, big hearts. Tellers of big, loving stories. The kind that kept us smiling long after the last piece of Gammie's Best Cheesecake was served.

I look down at an empty plate. Jessica has consumed all but one tiny strawberry, a lonely island in all that china whiteness.

"Slice number 24," I say to Jessica.

She reaches into her pocketbook and draws out her ledger, its corners folded over like paper napkins. She opens the ledger and lays it face down on top of the dessert plate with its patina of cheesecake and strawberries.

"I think it's time for the food ledger to go the way of corsets and girdles." Jessica smiles, the first time tonight.

"Should we order a second slice—to celebrate?"

Jessica pushes the spine of the ledger into the plate.

After Gammie's death, it took my mother several months before she could finally bring herself to sort through Gammie and Grandpa Jonathon's neat little house. Clothes and furniture to Goodwill. Porcelain figurines wrapped carefully in newspaper and laid in a trunk. My grandmother's life reduced to things inside cardboard boxes and plastic milk crates.

Aunt Clare and my mother divided up the Lennox. My sister Holly garnered Gammie's costume jewelry. I didn't want anything; I had memories to treasure.

My mother mailed me a cardboard box. I opened it carefully, folded back the tissue paper. Inside, all the colorful, cheerful recipe books that once lined Gammie's pantry.

And as I surveyed their contents, turning back the old covers, reading the penned inscriptions, running my fingers across the yellowed pages, I came across old friends. Familiar recipes, marked with a paper clip, a pressed corner, a scribbled star. Words in the margins: "Everyone raved over the stuffing. Christmas 1964." "Holly's favorite cookies, age six." "This cake celebrated Jonathon's promotion." And my name next to recipes for Cherry Pie and Chicago Fudge Cake.

I could almost smell the delicate scents drifting from the oven.

And then I saw it.

A recipe for cheesecake. Three pounds of cream cheese. Two cups of sugar. Five eggs plus two egg yolks. One half cup of heavy cream. And the four secret ingredients for Gammie's Best Cheesecake finally before my eyes.

Only it wasn't called Gammie's Best Cheesecake. It was called Chester's Famous Cheesecake. From Chester's of Broadway.

And below the recipe, in Gammie's even handwriting: "Our tenth wedding anniversary, 1939. Jonathon said this was the best in the world. I thought he was talking about the cheesecake. I didn't know he really meant his life with our girls. And me."

BORN AGAIN

Elizabeth Welles

 Our relationship traveled the worlds of our imaginations. We even dreamt the same dreams at night from far away places. We meditated at a guru's feet, laughed in cornfields, sneaking raw stalks into our mouths. We danced in the moonlight, talking till dawn. We sat in front of her Buddha surrounded by stuffed animal toys. It was romantic as in high adventure and personal discovery, dangerous living on the edge, even if it was only eating Mexican food and too many hot peppers.

We were twin souls and between us there were no hidden spaces until she said, "Christ is the way." She was born again on a November day.

Walking along a path in a state park, crunching over a gravelly road, we'd been aligned. In the instant it took for her to speak her Truth, the emotional ground shifted between us and I felt a deep cavernous abyss of difference. We stepped cautiously into this new terrain.

"Do you believe Christ is the *only* way?"

"Yes." She hesitated. "I believe in the Bible."

"What if you're born a Hindu, a Moslem, or a Jew?"

"Maybe with your dying breath you'll say 'Jesus' and be saved."

My cynical voice silently quipped:

Yes, maybe, and maybe you'll say Rama, Allah, God or Mother."

She continued. "Whatever happens in the privacy of a person's thoughts is between them and God. I pray my loved ones will be shown the way. We are taught to not put our complete faith in any living person on earth, even our pastor."

But you put your faith in a book, the Bible?

"And what do you think about the time we spent with the swami?"

"You won't like what I have to say, but I think it was the work of the devil. It steeped me in denial, bidding me away from Christ. Maybe I would have had a rebirth experience in Christ sooner. But I don't regret it. It brought me to where I am now."

I don't mind her evaluations. There were some seedy underpinnings to the swami but I wouldn't go so far as to call it the work of the devil.

Oh well, she found Christ. I never knew he was lost. I had many questions I didn't ask. *You said you do not put your trust in any man on earth but Christ was a man?*

"Blasphemy," I imagined a faceless authority striking back. "Christ was not a mere man."

Is most of the population condemned because they have not yet heard of a God-man who lived two thousand years ago? Those who die with something else in their hearts, minds, and on their lips, are they destined to a lifeless purgatory or an eternal hell?

I voiced this one aloud.

"What about all those who never heard of Jesus?"

"They're in ignorance." *(Meaning they're excused or unexcused? I clearly did not understand.)*

I sensed her awkwardness and mine, and so the thoughts rushing through my mind remained silent. This was an enduring friendship and I didn't want to be embattling. But behind her silence I felt judgment and a narrowness of mind that dismayed me. Obviously in her mind I had it all wrong, was still dillydallying around, off the mark or outright deluded.

"I will probably not talk with you about certain things," I said.

She understood.

"But the angels are still okay?" I asked.

"Oh, yeah, the Angels are fine," she answered.

My past with her felt obliterated. The once common ground we walked turned to sand beneath our feet. She was slipping away and I was in mourning. When a woman friend gets hooked into a serious and intimate relationship, other relationships often change. She clearly didn't need me. She had Christ. But I was also glad and didn't know why.

On the train back to the city I alternated between feeling free and angry. Slowly I realized I no longer needed or wanted the relationship the way it once was. A quiet, cosmic giggle blended with the sorrow, lightening the load. Although I felt loss, I felt released, secure, strong.

Then hot anger flooded me, and the question, "Why must one moccasin fit all the many feet? Religious or otherwise?"

I imagined her scorning what I was reading—Margot Adler's *Drawing Down The Moon*. I imagined her dismissing everything important to me: what I was doing and being, who I was. I thought of the "My way is the only way" mentality as a blockage, a wall, an arrogance reminiscent of a labeling system I loathed as a child, defining achievement by a letter A, B, C or D. Now we were defining destiny by belief—believe in Christ and you're saved. If not, go directly to Hell.

There are always others more or less proficient, I thought. Would it be possible to measure achievement while sparing the humiliation or burden of feeling lesser or greater? If we need to measure then let's look at the word *feedback* as "feeding back," nurturing. And if we nurture and honor the variety that exists among humans in all their ways of thinking and being, and in all their ways of celebrating the Divine, would the whole structure of "Church" come tumbling down? Or might the Church rise and expand to include infinite variety, to usher in and be one of the greatest vessels for peace on earth?

As we discover ways to nourish growth, respectful of differences, we open up our choices. Then, Oh my God, we might have freedom! Choice. A much talked about word today. Freedom: the exhilarated response to life that escorts us further into the unknown. Freedom: people stake their lives on it and fear it at the same time. No wonder we don't celebrate variety. Heaven forbid!

Secretly I wanted to tell my friend everything, if only for shock value. I wanted to shake her and wake her. I wanted to relive my trip to Japan for her and show her how people in another country worship and pray. I was a zealot from the other side rallying against her One Way. I respected her way but not her imposing it on the entire human race or me, even if she did it in the privacy of her thoughts. And when I had a break in my rallying, I mused with a chuckle, "My God, I'm doing the same thing I'm accusing her of. Where's the violence now?"

My mind twisted, turned and fought. Even if I was accurate in my perceptions, so what?

So what if the past was obliterated? It was after all the past, dissolving in the light of the Presence. The sand under our feet had once been ground that provided a nurturing base for our friendship. I could remember it with fondness for what it taught me without having to live there. Today I was dealing with a new friend—on new ground.

If I had a conversion experience, her church would welcome me with open arms. By my own admission I don't fit in. She finds solace in the Pentecostal way, singing Hallelujahs, speaking in tongues, fainting in the aisles. "Like an orgasmic experience," she once told me, she knows a peace in Christ, and I am glad she is fulfilled.

I love Christ and the Consciousness that attends His name. It is a Consciousness that belongs to all people irrespective of what it's called or of what we call ourselves. It is the same Love, Healing, Light, Peace, and Consciousness that attends the names of great prophets, sages, God-men and God-women who have graced this earth and that attends anyone, anywhere, when Spirit opens the heart. It is the same Living Spirit through Buddha and Ramakrishna, Mohammed and Moses, Christ and the Great Spirit. It lives through Kali and Quan Yin, in the Holy Mother and Mother Nature, and *most of all* in you and in me.

Although I disagreed with her belief in the *one and only way,* I recognized that I would defend her right to choose what she believes, and *that* understanding, *that* loyalty of spirit was more important than any agreement in philosophy we might ever come to. Still I sadly surmised we would not share as much with each other.

Then one evening when we were dining out, we were each given a plant. Mine died around the time she told me of her conversion, and I used the soil to nurture another plant badly in need of the earth. Then I turned to a book she so trusts in.

"In the Beginning God created the heaven and earth.
Now the earth was unformed and void..."

Perhaps there was another, yet unformed, way for us to be together, where we shared a peace from two seemingly contradictory views. We still laughed at the simple things, children's books, noises, a story of bad dreams spooking you in the dark.

"...And God called the light Day, and the darkness He called Night.
And there was evening and there was morning, one day."

Of course there was One Day, the Beginning. And I was being Born Again in the discovery of a new and different friend.

We live many miles from each other now, but the distance doesn't matter. Laughing on the phone we talk for hours. I know there is no One Way, as much as she knows there is. But it doesn't matter. We don't have to talk about it. That choice creates freedom for us to just *be* in our relationship.

When her son went to prison for five years, I wrote him. When my mother was rushed to the hospital for a life threatening illness, she was the first person I called to ask for prayer, and she continued to pray with me throughout the illness, sometimes at three in the morning.

Together we saw the movie, '*A River Runs Through It.*' Shortly afterwards I phoned and talked with her about voting for Clinton and not Bush.

"But Clinton isn't for gun control," she said.

I tried to explain that she had it backwards but her mind was made up. Clinton wasn't "pro-life" either. As we were hanging up, I reminded her of a line from the movie.

"As one of the characters says,

'We can love completely without complete understanding.'"

"That's right," she laughed—and the rest didn't matter.

OTHER MOTHERS

B. L. Wadas

 read a collection of works by Black women describing their relationships with their mothers. Initially I thought the book had nothing to do with me. The stories described warm, cozy, loving mother/ daughter relationships.

My relationship with my mother was in no way warm or cozy. My mother was an emotional infant. I estimate her emotional age at somewhere between two and nine years old. She was given to rages, depression and drink.

I do remember that she had a beautiful singing voice. My mother sang as she washed the walls of our project apartment. She was well spoken with beautiful diction. She might have been much different, had she been mothered. It is difficult to be a nurturing mother when one has been unmothered. My mother, Willie-Ruth, was an intelligent, angry woman who never had an opportunity to *be*.

She could not mother me as her *child. I learned to be quick, well behaved, independent and capable. I learned to be angry.* I used my anger to fuel my life. My anger/fear, fueled me through school and hard times. I used the sheer dint of my will. My will and my anger/fear stood me in good stead.

I learned to get my mothering from *other mothers* in the neighborhood. Miss Margaret did my hair and gave me my first grown-up sexy dress. Mrs. Wilson, my best friend's mother, included me in their family. Mrs. Wilson also taught me to groom my fingernails, keep my weight down and the boys' hands off me. I followed the Wilson family rules, regulations, for limits and behavior. I also got approval and affirmation from my teachers.

My mother could not mother me as a *needing her* child. It was not until I married, had children and divorced that my mother was able to *be there* for me. She could and did support me as the adult woman I grew into. Not only did she support me, she facilitated and admired me. I knew this and accepted what she had to give. She helped me financially when I returned to school. She baby-sat my children or sent my youngest brother to get my babies to give me a break. My mother *understood* and could relate to the pressure: my anger, my worries and problems as a *woman* raising children alone. She just could not mother me as a *needing her* child, the child *in* her absorbed what little energy she had. I forgive her.

I grew strong in her sight, in spite of her and because of her. Like my mother and her mother before her, I am full of contradictions.

MOTHER AND DAUGHTER
BEDMAKING

Karen Henninger

I stood on one side, she on the other
A distance, open area between us
Yet we were not at odds as I thought
The white flat sheet, unfolding
flung out into the air in front of my eyes.
As my mother's arms moved with the motion of dance
The sheet floated gracefully onto the bed.
We shared a likeness, we women
what we hated in each other we hated in ourselves
What we loved, we humbled. Passionately
Grasping the corners of the sheet we pulled from each other.
Folding the bottom, the side. Neatly. Smoothly.
Stepping to the head of the bed. Harmonious. Coordinated,
A well choreographed dance.

The art of bedmaking showed our practice
We didn't speak. Top and sides tucked in, the sheet lay flat
I don't remember the origins, instructions I must have been given
Sometime
She tossed a pillowcase to me.
I picked up the pillow that lay by my father's shoes.
And held it under my chin a split second before it fell
Through the opening of the case.
I laid the pillow on my father's side; it touched my mother's.
I knew they touched in a much different, private way.
I always knew she liked him better
I longed for the love she felt for him
We continued making that bed
and many more for sometime
But sometime, I don't remember when,
I began to make the beds alone
or perhaps with my little sister.
I don't remember the instructions I gave.
I only remember the synchronization of two women
preparing the beds for our family to rest.

SUNSHINE'S SMILE

Elizabeth Welles

After my Dad passed on, I missed him excruciatingly. So you can imagine my joy when, nine days after he died, he came to visit in a dream. Now my father—one of the most honest and compassionate people I've ever known—didn't believe in an after-life. So he wasn't the kind of person to come back in a dream to tell me something if it wasn't true, and he often came in humorous ways. I would say something to him and he'd answer back and have me laughing.

It was Easter Sunday, the day we were spreading his ashes. We didn't plan for that day specifically, it just worked out that way, and I liked it—the resurrection of Dad. Just that early morning, in the dream-state, my father was laughing and smiling. "If I only knew about this eternal life stuff," he said, just like that, "Like it would have been so much easier, who would have known. I saw Grandma, (my mother's mother,) the dogs, (her dogs) even Tippy," (one of her earlier dogs that died something like twenty years before.) He was chuckling over all the things we think and do around death. He looked well, happy, and real relieved. Dreams continued quite consistently through that first year. In another he said, "If you want, I'll help you with your writing, even everyday. I can help you with your writing, beautiful words and poetry, but you have to make an appointment because I'm very busy." He was happy to help, but he wasn't going to push anything on me. Even in life he wasn't a pusher of his ideas. In the dream, I found myself wondering, "Does he know he's dead?" Telepathically he heard my question and answered out loud in a funny off-handed way, "Yes I know I'm dead, but I'm not dead, and yes I know I'm not in the body, but I am in the body, right now, for you." A dear friend of my Dad's, who passed on six weeks after my Dad, came into the dream too. This friend had a heavier and more encumbered body when he lived on the earth. In the dream he walked into the house huffing and puffing from carrying all these packages. He looked at my Dad and telepathically voiced, "Oh boy, it's one helluva thing being back in these bodies," and they both giggled like little kids. It wasn't their number one priority—to be back in the body, but they were happy to do it for us right now.

I use to hear songs in my head totally out of the blue. I'd hear Stevie Wonder's "You are the sunshine of my life." Then one day I was in NYC walking the streets. It was a gray day and I was feeling low, really missing my Dad, when I heard… "You are my sunshine, my only sunshine, you make me happy when skies are gray, you'll never know Dear, how much I love you, please don't take my Sunshine away." I looked around to see if anyone was singing, I listened to hear if this song was playing anywhere nearby, I even peered into a store or two. And I'm thinking, "Dad?" My Dad loved music, loved concerts, classical and jazz, which I finally have begun to also love and appreciate, but the sunshine songs?

When he was very ill in the hospital he hadn't eaten for what seemed like weeks. One day he asked me for an apple.

I said, "Apple juice?" He shook his head no.

I said, "Apple Sauce?" He shook his head no.

He said, "Apple."

I said, "Oh an apple."

I happen to have brought a fresh apple from the house that day and had it in my bag. I ran to the nurse's station, got a knife and cut off a small portion of the apple, and from that portion I cut about seven tiny, baby-bird bite size pieces about half the length of a small pinky nail.

I began feeding these bird-size bites to my Dad, and as I was feeding him I said, "Here's a bit of sunshine Daddy, here's another little bit of sunshine." All I could think of was the sun shining down and nourishing these apples, making them healthy and whole, and of the sun shining through my father's whole body with each little bite. After about four bites, he put up his hand like a King and said, "It's all in," like he had just consumed the most sumptuous feast and was plentifully satisfied. Later as I held the urinal for him and his pee hit the side of the jug, he said, "Gravity, it's all in the gravity."

My father finally came home from the hospital for another six weeks of life. The day we brought him home, one of the nurses told us that none of the nurses had expected my Dad to leave the hospital. They use to come in each day, and say, "Oh Dan's still here!" The nurse felt it was a tribute to the family's care that he was leaving that day.

A week or so after we arrived home, we received a call from Marianne, a three-time cancer survivor herself, who had started an organization to help people with cancer and their families. What we didn't know was that she had stood in the doorway weeks earlier observing the apple interaction with Dad.

"I'm coming over, I have a present for you and your Dad," she said.

"What is it?" I asked.

"I'm not telling you, it's a gift."

I was on my way out for an appointment, but I waited. She arrived and we unwrapped the gift. My Dad's lying in bed with friends and family around, and she takes out this beautifully sculptured ceramic man with a yarmulke on his head, and a big bowl he holds in his lap with a little lid that comes off. On the bowl is written the words, "Bits of Sunshine for Daniel."

She said she was so moved by what she saw that she told an artist friend of hers who did this sculpture for us. The only requirement was that it had to sit where my father could see it. My father beamed.

"Oh, she's still feeding me Sunshine," he said.

The Tuesday before my Dad passed on, my mother and I took a break. My brother came over and watched my Dad for the evening, and my mother and I went to see Spalding Gray, the actor and monologist. When I came home, I told Dad about the performance and he said, "Why don't you be a storyteller," and he suggested I do it in California. I went upstairs and in the shower thanked God and my Dad, because it was one of the greatest gifts he could give me—to say pursue your dreams, do what you love, write, act, tell stories.

My Dad passed three days later, early Friday morning. The night before he died I remembered a dream I had of him weeks earlier. In the dream he was slipping down from his chair, and I was trying to pick him up. I called a friend in the dream and said, "Tiny, he's slipping away."

The day before he died was just like that dream. He was propped in a chair. I held his feet as each of us breathed. I breathed in, he breathed out. He breathed in, I breathed out. I was holding the feet of a Buddha, practicing breath, aware of our connection in the moment, and practicing for when we would breathe and receive each other's presence from "different" worlds. Later in the day, I was alone with him trying to make him comfortable, trying to help him sit up. I had eight pillows and two bolsters in back of him and he was still sliding down for he had absolutely no body strength. I called a friend that night from the bathroom with the door closed so I could cry and cry, and I said, "He's slipping away."

Friday morning came too early and my mother came upstairs to call me to help with my Dad. The night before she told me that he talked all night and at some point he said, "NO, NO, NO," and then "Okay, Okay."

I went outside, pointed my finger at the sky, and said, "If we can't keep him, then you take him with the greatest of love, peace, freedom, joy and enlightenment, and you better serve him well!!!" I went back inside and stroked his head, telling him he was beautiful and loved, how much we loved him, to focus on the love and his own natural rhythm, his own natural grace. At one point he reached out in front of him, like he was reaching for something and he said, "Where are we?" We said, "We're at home, you're in bed." Really I would like to have asked, "Where are you?" He reached out—and this was a man with no physical body strength left. He was trying to speak to us but it was hard to understand because he didn't have much saliva in his mouth and so I swabbed his mouth to get some moisture in it, his teeth locked, we got the swab stick out finally. My mother had gone to call my brother. She came back and said she didn't really know what to tell him, so I left to call him. I don't know why we kept leaving the room, there was a phone right there, but I guess we were being polite though it's funny, none of us had any illusions at this point, and he knew he wasn't getting better. I told my brother to come soon because it would be soon. My mother screamed for me just as I got off the phone. I hadn't been gone but for a minute or two. I ran and my Dad's eyes were open looking at my mom's but the expression was gone, they were blank. His last view was of her, and then he closed them. My mother kept saying, "Danny, you're not breathing, Danny, Danny, you're not breathing," then she turned to me, "What should I do?"

"Call Ricky," I said, and she left the room.

I jumped on the bed next to my Dad and while she was gone he took his last two breaths. If you've ever seen a person die, it can be rather dramatic or violent looking, not all the time, but sometimes. He took two deep gasping sighs. His whole body stiffened, his eyes rolled back, and then his eyes closed and his body relaxed. I was glad I was the only one to see that because to be honest I don't think anyone else in my family would want to have seen it, and I guess I wanted silence for my Dad, complete silence. I didn't even touch the body, I just wanted him to be free to leave without anyone pulling on him. I wanted him to have the greatest moment he could have for that enlightenment, that birth into Spirit. I remember thinking, "I didn't think it would be like this." It was so quiet, such silence in the room, and then after awhile I put my hand above his crown to feel his energy moving out, but I didn't feel anything. I'm sure he wanted to get out from his tired body as fast as he could, and so sky-rocketed out. I remember thinking I probably wouldn't even cry if my mother came back to the room and wasn't crying herself, but she was, and then I started. My brother was there in an instant. He told his four-year old son, Jeremy, to stay in the living room while he came in and cradled over the body with my mom. I went outside to pick grapefruit blossoms, then my brother brought his son in to kiss Papa's forehead one last time, like he did the night before when my father still breathed, the only time that day when my Dad smiled. My sister-in-law came over and then my beautiful nephew started handing out hats for everyone, including Papa. I appreciated Jeremy's ever-joyous nature and innocence, and yet as he put a beret on Papa's now silent head all I could think of was that movie, "Weekend at Bernie's," and I was like, get the hat off. My father loved berets and I'm sure he appreciated the moment. In fact there was a lot of humor that morning, along with the tears. My sister-in-law took Jeremy to school and my mother and brother turned to me and asked what I wanted to do. We took my Dad's pajama top off, I oiled his chest with a touch of scented oil and we wrapped him in a big white sheet. When we put the sheet around him, I lifted him up to get his shirt off, like I so often did in the weeks and days before. "He's so heavy," I said. My mother responded, "There's a word for that," and all I could think of was, "Deadweight?" Then his eye winked open and I said, "Look he's winking." We placed a column of flowers on his chest from his belly to his neck. My brother picked flowers from the garden, my mother used the rose in bloom next to the bed, and I had the white fragrant grapefruit blossoms. Then I lit a candle that would remain lit for the next two-and-a-half days.

My Dad left the body with his mouth open, perhaps it was those two gasping breaths. In any event, my mother kept saying, "Won't you close your mouth Danny? Won't you close your mouth?" And when I picked him up his mouth did close—for a second, but when I put him back down his mouth opened again. My brother and I said, "Mom he's not going to close his mouth," but she persevered. After a while we were all out of the room at the same time. I was in the driveway with the hospice nurse who finally arrived. It was incredibly windy, unusually windy, when suddenly I heard my mother calling me, "Come look, come see Daddy's smile, come see Daddy's smile."

My mother gets very enthusiastic sometimes, so I was thinking yeah, yeah, okay, when I'm done here. When I walked back into the room I could say it was a beatific smile that was on my Dad's face, but it was simply my Dad's smile, which was beautiful to us. My brother and I huddled together, lowered our voices and said, "That's Daddy's smile, that's Daddy's smile!" My mother said he heard us, and when we all left the room, his spirit came back into the body for a moment to close the mouth into his smile to say everything's Ay-Okay. My brother and I looked at the body, turning to each other at times to say, "looks like he's breathing." Even though he left the body, there was still so much life. We kept the body with us for seven hours and it was a most comforting time. We talked to my Dad, kissed him, and lay down beside him; the body was still warm. My sister-in-law sat by the bedside at one point, and said, "I know it sounds morbid, but can't we stuff him and keep him here?" It was that comforting. I did ask my mother if we could keep him a bit longer, but she said, "If we keep him any longer, we'll have him for the whole weekend." I guess I wouldn't have minded, feeling close to the Buddhist's three-day tradition of keeping the body. My mother gathered my brother and I in the kitchen and put her arms around us. Even with the obvious sadness and tears, she said she felt joy. I believe it was my father's joy that touched her. He was soaring through the clouds.

I finally called a dear friend to tell her that my Dad had passed. She returned the call several hours later and said, "I've got to tell you something. I was outside very early this morning, it was about the time your Dad passed, and I hadn't received your call yet. I closed my eyes to sort of connect with your family and your Dad, when I heard the most dignified and strong voice. It said, "This is Daniel. This is Daniel." I wondered what this was about, and then I realized it was Daniel, your father. He said, "Tell my most precious daughter I love her so very much, she has done so much for me. I am so glad you are coming; she needs you now. Tell her I am fine and she is going to be fine." My friend wondered was she making this up, she hadn't ever "channeled" before, or ever even tried. But then she got home, heard my phone message, and knew. She lay down for a moment and reconnected, "Anything else?" She asked. He reiterated what he said, and then added, "Tell her I am with her, tell her I am not leaving her. I am with her." He got out of the body as fast as he could and flew to my friend, whom he had never met, but knew I was close with, to give her that message.

All of us, in this Universe, interface with each other much more than any of us ever really know or perceive, in life and in the "hereafter." And in that place, that is beyond what we ordinarily "know," there is humor, peace, joy and love. My Dad's been with me ever since, as he has been with a whole lot of people, and the relationship continues. It's something few talk about, but many know. Relationships continue because love is profound and greater than death.

DANCING WITH MOM

Joy Jones

y sister and I snickered when our sixty-something mother decided to take ballet. We smirked when the dance instructor corrected her in front of the whole class as she bungled the routine. We hooted when Daddy said, "Your mother's gone crazy," once she quit cooking meals to be at the studio four times each week. We stopped laughing when we saw that her passion and discipline had transformed her matronly size fourteen shape into a chic size eight.

My mother, my sister Lorraine and I all had the same initial goal—let's lose weight. It was the eternal female battle against the spread of cellulite and the dread of thickening thighs. A dance class at a professional studio seemed like a good answer to the question: how can I eat whatever I want without gaining weight?

Dancing with my mother and sister blends the best parts of a twelve-step program and a fitness routine. I get to exorcise my frustrations and maybe drop a pound or two in the process. Our dance classes have saved lives. Not our lives, per se, although the exercise is good for decreasing the chance of heart disease and off-setting the damage done by our addiction to chocolate. No, our dance classes have probably saved your life. Remember when you changed lanes at the last minute and cut off the car behind you? That was me. What about that time you got into the express line at the grocery store with twenty-five items? I was the customer waiting behind you with the fifty-cent candy bar. Being able to work out my negative energy on the dance floor is what allowed me to stay calm and not curse you out on the spot. I know several supervisors who are still living and breathing today because dance class exists. And although my mother is retired and no longer has to answer to a boss, she has a thirty-year backlog of irritation from crazy supervisors that she is still working off.

For me, dance is a combination tension reliever and recreational sport. But Mom has something I don't have—the fire. I was surprised to learn that ballet was a secret desire she has harbored since girlhood. But the rural Kentucky of the 1930s and '40s where she grew up was not exactly a training ground for black ballerinas. College, marriage and career pretty much took up the succeeding forty years until she retired from teaching. Once she retired, she then had the time and still had the fire to pursue her childhood wish.

Whereas my sister and I—still working members of the rat race—can only squeeze class into our schedules once or twice a week, Mom has a dance regimen. She not only takes ballet, she also goes to two jazz dance classes a week and takes ballroom dancing as well. She checks out library books from the children's department that show beginning ballerinas how to position their feet. She practices dance combinations at home.

What's been eye-opening for me is to see my mother, a former teacher, become a student. This is a woman who taught—and terrified—third graders for thirty years. She was a strict disciplinarian in the classroom (and at home), your typical mean teacher. Now instructors who are younger than her own children call her by her first name. The woman who used to seat troublemakers at the front of the class where she could keep an eye on them, now hides in the back of the studio out of the instructor's line of vision.

You see, despite her fire, Mom has little skill. If dance were an academic subject, she'd be in the learning disabled group. Yet it's been amazing for me to watch her progress, to be the child witnessing the parent's growth. In the two years she has been taking lessons she has developed such grace, both physically and emotionally. She'll never be a Judith Jamison, but she has become a more beautiful Marilyn Jones.

I hate the fact that she's lost more weight than me, but I admire her zest and her daring, especially when I contrast her with so many of her peers who so obviously believe that "old dogs" can't learn new tricks. I admire her adventurous courage to try something new and demanding without fear of failure and no pressure to impress. She concedes that her dance skills are on the kindergarten level, but she doesn't dance to get a good grade or pass a test—just for the sheer pleasure and challenge of it all.

Now if only we could get Daddy in a pair of leotards!

CHAPTER THREE

THE GIFTS OF TRAVELING THROUGH TIME

Breath of Life
that breathed me onto the earth,
help me to seek within this cycle of birth
the breath that fills all and inspires us to live,
and bridges the gaps between today's and tomorrows
between our joys and our sorrows.

WE REALLY HAVE COME
A LONG WAY

Evelyn Kellman

 My mother and her two sisters took turns having the big Thanksgiving feast. It was before frozen foods or microwaves or dishwashers, when the concept of "bought" pies were not to be mentioned in polite company.

My aunts worked full time, commuting three hours to New York City. It was the Depression and they were supporting their husbands. My mother cared for my grandmother and did piecework to keep us financially afloat while my dad regularly looked for work that would pay more, or sometimes just looked for work.

The routine was for the women to gather on Wednesday night after work to prepare the stuffing, the vegetables and the relish tray. (They drew straws to see who would peel the onions.) The shopping had somehow been fitted in during the week. No one knew about vitamins, so the pared vegetables sat on the porch in pots of water. They hadn't heard about salmonella, either, so the "bird" was stuffed and also went on the porch. One sister would have baked three kinds of pie whenever she could fit it in and Frankie would give her plum pudding a final lacing of rum.

Next morning the turkey was put in early—6:00 a.m.—lest the gas pressure go down. The pressure was something they always talked about but it never went down that I remember. I guess it was part of the ritual.

The table was set with the best linen and dishes, Grandma's cut glass and the silver-plate. Ironing boards were stretched between chairs for extra seating, and card tables set up for the overflow. It was a given that the house had been "fall cleaned" with newly stretched curtains, washed windows, laundered doilies on polished furniture and waxed floors. The women had done this nights and weekends.

While the turkey cooked, what hadn't been prepared the night before got done. There was white sauce for the onions, Aunt Rene's ice cream sauce for the pudding, bacon to be fried to go over the beans, bread crumbs toasted for garnish, parsley washed and "sprigged" (not chopped, thank you!), yams candied.

Finally when the bird was taken out to rest, gallons of mushroom gravy were made from the vegetable liquors, pan drippings and flour. The jar in which the flour was blended invariably blew its top or slipped out of the shaker's hands making an awful mess. It was finally decreed that forevermore the "shaker" had to go out to the yard to shake—rain or shine.

The trick was to get everything ready and kept hot without losing flavor so that when the men and guests were seated and had their appetizer, the turkey could be borne in and placed ceremoniously before the host for carving.

The women were expected not to come to the table in their kitchen clothes, so somewhere midst the flurry they changed into "something presentable." Between replenishing bowls, bringing hot gravy and more cold cider from the porch, they got to eat their meal.

The main course done, dishes were removed and stacked wherever room could be found in their tiny kitchens or on the porch. Dessert became the next order of concern. Who'll have mince, who for pumpkin, plum pudding? Both? All three? Ice cream? Whipped cream? Hardsauce? Some of each? Andy, you're a glutton! How many coffees? Tea? Black? Cream?

And so it would go until everyone was stuffed beyond comfort. The women left the table and headed again for the cramped kitchen. The men lingered, smoking holiday cigars, making jokes about who was the worst glutton, who was the fattest—Andy or John. They complained about FDR's "socialism" and especially about that pushy Eleanor. They didn't like his Secretary of Labor, "Ma" Perkins, either.

Finally they would adjourn to the living room to the overstuffed horsehair chairs to listen to the football game on the radio. But mostly they napped.

A long time would pass before the women finished the piles of dishes and dealt with the leftovers (on the porch again). Packages and jars were made for each family to have a "leftover" dinner. Then they would join the men to hear the annual argument of who had napped and who had snored the loudest and the latest prizefight controversy.

Then it would all begin again. One of my uncles would say, "I can't believe it, but I'm hungry again—how about some sandwiches?" That didn't mean he was offering to make them.

The turkey sandwiches had to be on fresh baker's bread (one sister made the early morning trip to the bakery). White? Dark? Cranberry? Stuffing? Mayo? Salt, pepper? Heaven forbid someone should get something he didn't like. Cider? No, you want coffee? Black, cream, tea, seltzer? Pumpkin, mince, cake… Dishes again. Finally around 9:00 p.m. folks would leave.

Looking back, I can't remember hearing the women ever complain about the imbalance of chores, though they were exhausted, and I know I never heard the men suggest that they take over any of it. After all—they carved!

For years I wondered about that. These were certainly not bad men, nor were the women stupid. It was as though they were caught in a tableau each playing an assigned role. Even to a child, the inequality was obvious.

GOD THROUGH BASEBALL

Tamara Engel

s a therapist I get to share in people's private thoughts—their sexual fantasies, more private thoughts—the state of the art of their checkbooks, and their most private thoughts—their relationship with their spiritual realm or as one patient said, "You should excuse the expression, God." What initially surprised me is how for many people their positive emotional connection to someone or something beyond themselves was not found in the places their parents sent them for their "religious education," but instead found them serendipitously in the guise of riding and tending horses at a summer camp, working in a vegetable garden or even being a fashion model. I came to God through baseball.

Baseball was my first oneness experience. While some of my friends walked to shul with their fathers on Saturday, I walked with my father twenty-two blocks up Bedford Avenue to the wild and wiles of Ebbets Field. When we entered the stadium it was dark. The long tunnel to reach our seats was even darker. But if we persevered, and we always did, the magnificence of the sun shining on the green grass, rust dirt and white lines always left me feeling that I was as close to heaven as I had ever been. I rooted for the Dodgers, my father despite living in Brooklyn his entire life, quite unnaturally to me, favored the Giants. In the ball park we could both assert our independence.

I loved to cheer with the crowd when Gil Hodges got his man out at first, stand up in unison when Jackie Robinson hit a home run or stole another base, collectively groan when a ball went right through short stop Pee Wee Reese's legs, ritually stretch at the middle of the seventh inning, and even cry with everyone when our Campy and our picture of him as permanently crouched at homeplate was shattered. I was part of something bigger than my life—even bigger than Brooklyn.

When the Dodgers won the pennant, which they did a few times, I became excited about the World Series. I was even more excited if it was a subway series not between but against the Yankees. Then everyone came out of the woodwork and out of themselves. The otherwise dour and sour mom and pop grocer posted inning by inning scores in their store window. There was a "pool" in my father's factory; he was in it and there was a chance he would win money. Kids brought radios to school and even the stern teachers allowed us to listen. The best of them didn't give homework because they understood and compassionately knew we were otherwise involved.

Time became timeless, I became you, you became me, Brooklyn became the world and God was good and everyone had their double portion. When the Dodgers lost the series, as they usually did, my grief was shared and "wait until next year" was our password, our mantra and our prayer for redemption and hope. When they did win the series in 1955 I went to my first and only tickertape parade along Flatbush Avenue. Flatbush Avenue was the still point of the turning world and summer preternaturally extended itself that year.

In 1957 when the Dodgers left Brooklyn for who cares where, I was bereft. Where would I find the Divine? Happily I've found it; more precisely it finds me. But if truth be told, loyalty is loyalty, and God is a Brooklyn Dodger. An enlightened being can't be one without knowing what e.r.a. and r.b.i. stand for and eternal means that diamonds are forever.

COMING OF AGE – KANSAS CITY 1970

Pat Huyett

Our folks thought we'd bummed rides
back to college; instead we stayed
crosstown at the Ecstatic Umbrella.
Grace Moreno drove.
We stopped at the
Ramada Inn parking lot.
Ram it all in, Connie said.
Snow dissolved on the windshield.
Two nights before
the Doc turned us away
for not bringing cash.
What Connie had come for
turned out cheaper
underground in Missouri
than legal in Kansas.
Connie wore a peacoat and
my tie-dyed skirt for its drawstring,
soft against her tender middle.
Gracie said, "Don't worry,
he's a real doctor."
I said, "And remember, you both
had the clap and took lots of drugs."
Gracie handed her the envelope
with the two hundred a rich
feminist had given us.
Then the Lincoln pulled up,
Connie clicked open the door,
and with the cold against
our faces, Gracie told her
"Go with God."

BREAKFAST SANDWICH

Marilyn Gelman

He was your standard, old-fashioned regulation-type creep. His blue suit was right on the button, his white shirt was as clean and pressed at the end of the day as at the beginning, and he wore the power-color tie appropriate for each year. But he was a thorough creep.

Riding the rails in the early eighties was an exercise in sexual harassment. Accepted by both men and women, it was part of the daily routine and almost invisible. But this man went beyond catcalls, coughing and the obvious out loud appraisals. Early one morning this man and another commuter made me the filling in their "breakfast sandwich." Pressed tightly and rubbed, I was enraged, entangled and claustrophobic. I considered my options from shouting to stomping, but the 1982 reality was that any action I took would cause a group reaction of ridicule. I would hear comments and snickers every morning for weeks. So I gripped the seat handle, grit my teeth and became a cooperating victim. The next day I saw the pre-game maneuvering and eye-contact between the creep and another man, but I was too late to escape.

If nothing else, commuters are creatures of habit. We know the exact spot on a platform where the train doors will open and we know who is fleet of foot and who is faint of heart. We develop our patterns according to a very personal set of choices or balances: a seat in a back car or standing room in a front car to insure an earlier connection, a quiet car where even the newspapers are turned without a rustle, or a party car for kibitzing over a cup of morning coffee. These habits, which make it possible to transport so many people in so little time, permit us to gracefully and efficiently dance our roles in a daily choreography, which can last for years.

On the third morning, when the men were waiting to pounce again, I took the only choice I saw—I altered my commuting pattern. The change impacted the time I left the house, the place I parked my car, crowd conditions during travel, breakfast, and the amount of time I could spend with my kids each day. Because these adjustments were due to someone else's agenda, not mine, I traveled each day with rage. I overreacted to casual crowding. I wrote letters to employers about controlling workers who were cultural harassers.

Months later a woman offered me the fourth seat in a two-facing-two arrangement on a homeward bound train. Because he was one of the trio already in place, I rejected her offer and whispered, "He's a creep." She nodded and laughed.

Like many of the two hundred thousand rail and bus commuters who cross the state line each day in search of the pot of gold, I liked to include a breakfast stop as part of my journey. My restaurant was tucked in a corner of the busy main concourse of the World Trade Center. It served four hundred breakfasts daily, but to its regular customers it had the flavor of small-town America.

One day I shared my table with another regular, a classy brassy gal. She was slender, tough and tanned with a deep voice and a loud, fast, biting manner of speech. As she finished her breakfast and prepared to leave, I spotted the creep joining the cashier's line. For the first time, I told the full story of the train incidents.

"Oh yeah?" she said; then my street-smart buddy joined the line behind him. I don't know what he did to her. Maybe he faced her and undressed her with his eyes; maybe he brushed against her or leaned on her. Maybe he snorted, groaned, or made kissing sounds. Whatever it was, she turned to me and silenced the restaurant by booming, "You know, you're right! He is a creep!" The stillness was the loudest I could ever imagine. It had the impact of a bomb. No one laughed; no one snickered. Her shout was that of a fighter, not that of a victim. The times had changed enough for her to cry "foul."

The creep and I continue to cross paths. In our community, we glance blindly through each other; in the city, we lock eyes in the knowledge that we know the score; and on the train, when he's sitting in the midst of a trio of women, or closing in on a standee, I stare him down—daring him to make a move on anyone. How sad to be a creep in the late eighties.

What of the young women, the girls who blossomed during this decade of our adolescence? Perhaps I saw the harbingers of things to come during a lunch hour in the business district one early spring day. The young women wore well-tailored suits, in business fabrics, of a masculine quality and a feminine style. Whether the heels of their shoes were high or low, the women had the confident gait of people accustomed to the pace. They stood with their hands in their pockets and their heads thrown back in full-bodied laughter. No clones of young men, the women seemed like graduates of the right schools; team players, athletes, prepared for the business world; exuding excitement, good health, and anticipation.

Only time will tell if these women will be kept from the corporate suite or the executive washroom; but at least we know that, as of now, these crusty gals won't be the filling in anybody's breakfast sandwich.

Taking Off and Landing –
a New Narrative

Judith Beth Cohen

"In nineteenth century novels they get married. In twentieth century novels they get divorced. Can you have an ending in which they do neither?" Erica Jong

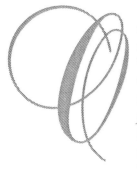n a plane lifting off from Cincinnati on the cusp of my fiftieth birthday, I search for narratives of female sexuality that tell my story, but I find none. Where can I read about a menopausal woman with two lovers, each of whom knows of and accepts the other's existence. The dominant culture says this can't work. At my age, I will be abandoned for younger flesh; I can look forward to hot flashes, a dry vagina, a depleted sex drive. Haven't media stars Germaine Greer and Gail Sheehy warned of the terrors of this midlife passage? Yet both my lovers are five years younger— they could find other women. Traditional plots would have me punished for my pleasure. Psychiatry would label my behavior as denial ("You may think this is fun but you're only running from death or worse.") And militant feminists would call me retrograde for loving men.

Yet I'm fresh from two delicious nights at an old inn with my lover. The hours were thick with intimate talk, with stories and poems read aloud, tales of our post-divorce lives, failed and successful seductions, secrets I've told only women—that loose free-form stream that follows no linear order, yet feels so full, so exhilarating. We solve work problems, share teaching ideas—can this be? A mid-life lover who has the body of a virile man and the sensibility of a literate woman? We've been meeting monthly for more than a year and have only begun to explore the exquisite reciprocity of pleasure. Our room is redolent with almond massage oil and body scents. I wear and discard the wonderful silk slip and lace panties he's given me. We, who thought we'd lived so much, are astonished to find sex fuller, richer, more intense than ever, but we agree that our passion could not thrive in the daily routine of our lives. We create a time and place for this ritual celebration of ourselves and sex.

When my plane lands, I will go home to the man I live with, who welcomes me with loving hugs. He's full of his own life and productive in my absence. I return to the familiar warmth of our shared bed and comforting rituals. We will cuddle under the electric blanket, my body encased in a flannel nighty, our cat purring on his chest, each of us reading our separate books. Later in the dark, we'll reach for one another under the quilts, discard our winter garments and make love. It may not be as slow and luxurious as sex with my lover, yet it is rich and satisfying, reaffirming our love.

Twenty years ago, I read *Fear of Flying,* raw from a failed marriage in which we lived like rival siblings, better at jousting and quibbling than loving. My head was full of fantasy lovers like Jong's zipless fuck. I would be overcome by lust, swept away by the man's powerful passion, bearing no responsibility for my own sexuality. But such men were disappointing and self-absorbed, such fantasies, the creation of a male culture that equates force and violence with passion.

For many years, I lived alone with long stretches of celibacy, and short spurts with ridiculous lovers—men I settled for from boredom or a need to reassure myself. My emotional and intimate life was with women—my erotic life with myself, played out in masturbation fantasies. A long sexual fast forced my appetite to shrivel, while the cultural narratives of rescue and fulfillment with one ideal lover still drove me. Twenty-nine-year-old Isadora Wing imagined having a harem of three husbands, but she couldn't do more than move from lover to husband searching for herself in the other.

At twenty-nine I was like her—at forty-nine I slid over the hump of middle age, and came to sexual maturity. My erotic side, suppressed and malnourished for so long, flourishes. I experience love that is not based on possession or exclusive ownership. With each man I ride the crest of holding and the trough of letting go. Each of us has an independent life—we don't grasp the other for completion, but expansion. My story has no conventional ending, no "happily-ever-after," no forced choice, no winners or losers. To ask: "why two if you have one good one?" is to echo a patriarchal assumption. To those who would send me to a shrink, I suggest the shrinks might learn from me.

Jong wrote: "I think we have too little genuine permissiveness... and too much bureaucratic disorganization masquerading as permissiveness. Real permissiveness, constructive permissiveness is another story altogether."

And it's a story that should be told. It's not about self-indulgent pleasure, but rather about going beyond the counter dependent dyad to new forms of intimacy and connection.

My tale is no utopian fantasy—loving more than one is not only possible, but better. I have intimacy without monogamy. I have love with more than one without deception or secrecy. I have collaborators with whom I create this new text—this circular story with no linear plot that goes on and on, returning again and again to the room at the inn, the hours in bed, the words gushing out, the best lubricant of all.

AT TWELVE WITH AL

Kara Manning

 l Pacino spit on me from the stage of "American Buffalo" when I was about twelve. Whether that moment blessed upon me the love of theatre or something more questionably Freudian in my forthcoming relationships with men, I'm not entirely certain. But I did know that when Al walked on stage my life changed. Twelve and teetering on the soft sand that sighs under your feet in the tide by the sea. Pacino. I hadn't even gotten my period yet, but I felt the flutterings of love in my heart. "Serpico." "Dog Day Afternoon," the words "Attica, Attica" on my lips. Michael Corleone. That long camelhair coat. Bobby Deerfield. I even accepted Al as boring Bobby Deerfield. This was no ordinary crush. This was total acceptance of Al.

I don't think my mother accepted my Al enthrallment as blithely as I did. Something about me dying to see Al's first movie, "Panic in Needle Park," made her a little edgy. Something about being at a David Mamet play—fuck you, no fuck you, no FUCK YOU—had her even edgier. But it was my birthday. And it was my only request. To see Al in the flesh.

I suppose she understood. In her day, she had Sidney Poitier. My mother loved Sidney Poitier and I loved her for that. It's inevitably cool when your mother defies race barriers in the '50s by simply having a crush. She told me once, when she was in her art school-beatnik-black capri pants and little ballet flat days, that Sidney Poitier walked by the glass window of the Greenwich Village coffeeshop where she used to hang out. My mother, all pixie haircut and slender French cigarettes. Sure. Since when. She must have been hallucinating. But Sidney Poitier strode down Bleeker Street and my mother followed. Right out the door. Down Bleeker Street, crossing to Cornelia and then several blocks further. He disappeared—walked up the stairs of a brownstone, knocked on the door. My mother stood there on the sidewalk, all Audrey Hepburn innocence, and tried to choke out a shuddery hello. Sidney turned from the doorway, saw my mother, nodded slightly and smiled a smile that dazzled my mother to the core of her beatnik soul. "Sidney smiled at me," she marveled. "Sidney smiled." The door of the brownstone opened and he disappeared inside, lost to my mother forever.

Yes, movie star crushes are not meant to be sane things. Yet my mother laughed at me when I turned a whiter shade of pale and grasped her arm when Al shuffled on stage. She was marvelously understanding. Having your prepubescent daughter doe-eyed over a scruffy actor who's played a mob boss, heroin addict and bank robber isn't necessarily a good thing, as Martha Stewart would say. But it was there. And when Al did spit in my direction, a long caring, wad of saliva soared over four rows to gently sprinkle over me like an April shower, I wasn't repulsed. It was probably my first truly sexual moment, all that Freudian stuff aside. I felt it was as good as a blessing from some psychopathic pope. A blessing for the last passage, the last journey, the last year you have as a child shifting into womanhood.

But when you're twelve years old, you don't think that way. You're allowed to suspend reason and drape it from your window like a ragged flag. Twelve is sitting in a circle with your four best friends on a July twilight, passing around a single cigarette stolen from an older sister, coughing profusely and pointing out the constellations in the sky to one another. Twelve is taking ballet class and one afternoon, somewhere between a glissade and a jété, staring in the mirror and realizing you have breasts. Twelve is BLT sandwiches and long-distance love affairs with the idea of living in London. Twelve is coltish crushes on skinny boys named Sam, outrunning one of Janet Palmetier's five brothers, and penciling poems under a willow tree. Twelve is galloping a chestnut quarter horse across an open field and singing "Can't Help Falling in Love" at the top of your lungs. Twelve is as sturdy as a young maple tree, shaking its leaves at the wind, willing to bend right or left, or left or right. Twelve is the edge of the abyss, twelve is the last great hope. Twelve is a visit to New York, drinking hot chocolate at the Palm Coast in your best black velvet dress and still wishing to watch the ice skaters at Rockefeller Center. Twelve is before Madonna, AIDS and 90210 existed as anything other than Christ's mother, a dietary candy and a zip code. Twelve is a single candle held in the air on St. Lucia Day, solid in Scandinavian spirituality, lost in a shuffle of snow and December coughs. Twelve is young and free and fresh and ultimately final. Nail in the coffin, another nail in my heart, it's the murmur and shuffle of coats before the play's begun.

You can sense the change coming, you can feel it pinch your toes and muss your hair. And the moment Al Pacino spits on you in "American Buffalo" in a not too pretty moment, the bile and bite of the real world spins you 'round and 'round 'til you can't catch your breath.

MIXED SIGNALS

Elizabeth Welles
(a monologue)

remember the first time I asked my mother about 69, well it was the first and last time. She was driving the car, and I thought we were headed for an accident. Her body tightened up and she stiffly said, "Draw it." So I drew it in the air with my little eleven-year old hands, and quietly said, "Oh." I got it. Then she asked where I had heard about it from and I said, "Jane," a friendly acquaintance from school. I don't think she much approved of Jane after that. And nothing was ever said again.

Well 69 became big. Marlena, an upper classman, took it upon herself to instruct the girls in the class below how to do it real well. The Martha Stewart of Sex. So we all became experts. Did it before we lost our virginities, kind of like the carriage before the horse I suppose, but from that alone, men would fall in love with us, well Jake did.

Valentines day, big man on campus with a big reputation, I was about 14, still lived at home, but knew all the guys at the local frat. He wanted to be my boyfriend, but I got too scared and backed away. Never heard any rumors about me, like all the others he was with, he respected me.

I don't know if it was sex in general with my mother, getting her needs met or communicating about sex. But these topics we didn't broach and by the time she was ready, I was way ahead of the game and didn't want to hear anything from her. I remember when she touched herself, you know just as people touch themselves unconsciously. Here was a sensuous woman who was so confused, passing on double standards to her daughters. Being asked why we didn't go out on more dates, and being told to pull our shirts down because we'll excite men, you know the midriff shirts we use to wear. But I don't think it began with her, this inability to communicate, I think it was an ancestral sort of thing born out of the unhappy union of grandparents who split up shortly after her arrival. When I asked my Grandmother her thoughts on marriage, she said,

"Stay single, you're better off," and then she added, "Eh, do whatever makes you happy."

At 17, I sat in a darkened theatre with this man who also touched himself—well not touched himself, but rubbed his arm or chin or chest. A flood of feeling exploded over me, and I wanted to touch him and be touched by him, but I hardly knew him, I was turned on and raw, and wanted to say, "Stop that! You're distracting me from the acting," and "No, no, go on, I am grooving on your sensuous ways," and that first night when I was with this man? When we just went to the theatre and had a drink? I lost words. Pretty remarkable, huh? I didn't know what to say for fear of sounding stupid, a complete imbecile, yet he was attracted *to me,* with movie moments of awkward silences and pregnant pauses. I wanted the sky to cave in or to go back to when I didn't care, when I didn't care about him.

He dropped me at the 14th street subway stop, across from the Chemical bank, and was about to take my head in his hands and kiss me, when I said, "I don't know." I don't even know why I said I don't know, he didn't ask anything—it just came out of my mouth, but he was intuitive and easy, and said, "Okay, let's experiment," and there was no going back. There were the floodlights from every movie and every train station meeting with your loved one after war, and I heard music that wasn't there—all because we were smashing teeth. And I just hate this human stuff, I hate it. You're kissing the one you love and you're so happy you can't stop smiling while you're kissing. *(She raps her nails against her teeth.)* And so your teeth are knocking into each other and it doesn't matter because you're in bliss, and you break a tooth—and the doctor discovers a lump in your gum—and is it benign or malignant? Just when you're having a good time, you can't die now, no, not now, and of course it's just a bump from having bitten yourself so hard. I mean you just love this person, this happening, this moment, the day, life—and then—then you're at the 24-hour grocery store stuck between split peas and lentils and you're wondering do they love me? I don't want commitment, but what if they leave or find someone better? I don't see anything in me, what do they see? Do they love me—will they leave me? I mean there's got to be a middle place. They'll love and leave me—so who cares? That's it, not caring, not giving a flying hoot about what happens, just live, *and die!* But, maybe *(pause)* all this kissing and smashing of teeth—I mean loving so much has got to take you someplace better, right? *(Long pause.)* There's so much confusion over death anyway. Basically there is more or there isn't more. Now if there's not more, there's no trouble, that's like a dead end, and so let's take the preferable tact of there is more. Then there's what do you do and where do you go when you get over there. Christians have it basic; it's heaven, hell and purgatory. I heard they use to have a limbo, but that got lost. For Buddhists it's a little more complicated—it's turn left at the blue light, dodge the green, go directly to the yellow. It gives me a headache. I just hope they have traffic cops or signals up there, because there could be a lot of accidents. There are just so many dictates for how to live—there's so manly dictates for how to *die,* that you wonder how to do anything at all?! I hate this human stuff. So chew a little, take a bit in, digest a little, get that saliva mixed up, like kissing, and then spit it out and skip the rest. Do a little loving, taste a little life, have a few experiences while here and don't get too involved!

A blind date once took my hand while watching the food scene in the Big Night: pasta and burgundy, pork and port, risotto and ravioli. I thought I was going to die, and they kept saying that in the movie, that the food, great food would kill you. But it never did. I couldn't even concentrate on the movie anymore and I loved the movie up to that point. I was so bummed. I was smiling ear to ear watching the people dance and eat, and now he's playing with my fingers. And I'm usually good focusing my attention in two places at once, but I just couldn't do it—all I knew is that he had my hand—no wonder my mother couldn't focus on driving and 69, too much of a split focus, a split diversion!

I don't know how my parents did it. They say they can't stand the movies with all the sex in them, they don't want to be in someone else's bedroom. One day we were watching this great, great love story on TV, and the love scenes come on, you know the HBO uncut version, and my mothers suddenly gets up and leaves, suddenly. Well that threw a wrench into the rest of the scene, because it was like she was mad. When my five-year old asked me about sex, admittedly I was a little shocked, but before he asked, he said, "Now don't be mad at me." I asked, "Why would I be mad at you for asking?" And he said because all the other mommies at school got mad at their kids for asking. Well I did the age appropriate thing, said two sentences, and then he wanted his juice. So now I went into the kitchen after a bit to get some popcorn, and she's coming out of the bathroom, her eyes are red, and she's quite shaken. I want to ask, "What happened?" But I almost don't want to know. Then she briefly says, "Its been a long time ago for me and your Dad," the age appropriate thing to her oldest daughter. And I think she now wants to ask me, "What happened?" You know, with the movie—like what did she miss? A lot. She has missed a lot! But I don't want to talk about it. That's what she did and that's what I'm doing. I hope I'm better with my kids, but who knows. Maybe you shouldn't give all the answers, tell a little lie, save some of those goodies, and certainly don't discuss it! If they ask me about 69 when I'm headed for a green light, it might be a dead stop. So if you're in back of us, watch out. And if it's a red light, maybe I'll drive right on through, keep on going, break those rules, ask questions. What's 69? A number!! Legal in some states, illegal in others.

Mixed Signals. Maybe they're just a part of life.

DAUGHTER OF A STOCKBROKER

Lyn Lifshin

I knew nothing about
AIDS when she
was in high school
and persuaded her
boyfriend to stop
using condoms
in favor of the
pill. All I
worried about
was getting pregnant.
Now I'm 24, I found
out I was HIV positive
when my boyfriend
died of the virus
a month after
his own diagnosis.
We were all 19
years old, nothing
like this was
supposed to happen
to us. Our biggest
worry was supposed to
be what outfit
to wear the
next day. I gave up
plans to be a
lawyer when my T-cell
count began to drop.
I've rallied, with
help of friends.
Sir, I'm white,
heterosexual,
from the suburbs—
but, for those
struggling with the
disease, differences
melt away.

PURSES

Ellen Blais

few years back I decided to stop carrying purses. After forty-odd years of collecting, worrying over, forgetting, juggling, figuring out where to put the damn things, I got myself a small, slim velcro bill-fold, jettisoned the billfold family pictures, and wore only clothes with pockets to accommodate a billfold and small change.

I felt light, I felt free. Walking, I swung my arms in healthy, energetic arcs and felt smug when I saw my less-enlightened sisters hauling around their ball and chains. For a very brief time—a matter of days —I sensed something was missing and looked around for a purse I didn't have. But quickly, I felt as free as the two or three-year-old me who skips purseless through the early family albums.

Perhaps six months into my new *modus vivendi,* I regarded the purse collection still in my closet. I thought I might be ready to get those nuisances out of my life complete-ly. What do you do with a purse you no longer want? I could throw away an old, bat-tered purse, but these purses were still in their prime. There were the winter purses: mid-sized, sturdy leather shoulder bags, brown and black for everyday, and for the evening a snazzy red leather clutch to match my red heels. And summer purses: a small Chinese cotton zippered shoulder bag, a slightly larger canvas shoulder bag with burgundy trim, a straw job with a flop-over top. And the fanciest of either season: a small "opera" bag, black-cloth lined, with beige tapestry material on the outside, in a multi-colored floral design over a black background. An admirer of the old school had gotten it for me on a trip to Vienna, but I never really went anywhere quite up to its standards. Well, I certainly had to keep that one. It was almost a work of art. But everything else could go. I thought.

Purses aren't really burnable in the normal sense, although I briefly entertained the idea of a gasoline-soaked pyre somewhere on the edges of our woods. The logical thing was to give them away, but I couldn't quite see myself dumping them en masse into the Salvation Army bins. Not in broad daylight, at least. So it must be the garbage. One at a time, I would put them in the small garbage can under the sink, until they were all gone.

I picked the business-like brown shoulder bag and gingerly laid it on top of the garbage. I went about my business, but an image of the dumped purse kept arising, unbidden. It didn't seem right to send something so good and faithful on its way to the compactor and the landfill.

Sheepishly, I rescued it and put it back on the shelf in the closet. I should have known something was going on, when the purses seemed too personal to give away. They were me. They were the equipment I took out to face the world. They had given me something to cling to in uncomfortable social situations. When they matched my shoes, they were a sign of my stylishness, my savoir faire. They were my woman-ness. No matter how short my hair, no matter how baggy my jeans, they signaled my gender to a world where this is the first thing one notices about someone—before race, before age, before physical equipment. I might not be using them any more, but that didn't mean I could just throw them out. Any more than I would have a hysterectomy just because I was no longer ovulating.

I got to thinking about women and purses, me and purses, and found the forgotten purses of my past tumbling through my mind. There was my grandmother's black handbag with its gathered leather top and metal clasp. I don't think I ever saw her out in the world without some form of this handbag dangling from her right hand, a detachable appendage. There is a picture of the two of us when I was four and she was in her fifties. My mother labeled it "Sunday Pals," for we are headed off to church. Gran wears a short fur jacket over a ruffled blouse and loosely gathered wool skirt. I wear a wool tam, light-colored, and a dark wool coat. Gran holds a pair of dark gloves in the hand which is not around my shoulder, and from that hand hangs a shiny leather purse, light gleaming from the creases and bulges of its gathered top. I have one much smaller, but similarly creased and gleaming. Eighteen years later, in my college graduation picture, she is shorter than I, and I'm carrying no purse, but Gran has hers, held in her right hand, a white leather summer handbag matching her white, open-toed, low-heeled grandmother shoes.

Gran never had a shoulder bag, as I remember, nor did she have purses in any but the basic black, white and tan colors. But my adventurous Aunt Dorris introduced a turquoise leather drawstring bag sometime in the '50s, and she had the first shoulder bags I remember seeing.

Shoulder bags were a significant change in purse technology, probably paving the way for the sexual revolution of the sixties. Beats and hippies sported shoulder bags. They are less hampering as they swing unheld from the shoulder. One's hands are free, one's arms not weighted down.

I don't remember carrying a purse to school when I was still in the elementary grades. I came home for lunch, and the milk money I took was knotted in a handkerchief or, in winter, slipped into my glove.

Junior High was probably when I started making purses a regular part of my daily attire. Just about the time of my first menarche, in fact. I remember how important it was at that stage not to let a boy get hold of your purse or inadvertently drop it and expose the contents, which frequently included a bulky Kotex modestly wrapped in kleenex. By high school, boys begin to see purses as one of the feminine mysteries, a taboo holy of holies they desire but fear having possession of. I lived in terror of dropping my purse and spilling its sacred contents at the feet of some grinning, pimply adolescent male.

In college I carried a green book bag in lieu of a purse, but I still maintained a suitable collection for more formal occasions. Then, when I started teaching in the late sixties, I began sloughing off my feminine symbols—the bra, the make-up. But the purses were the last to go. Now that I think about it, I didn't give them up right until around the time that my periods stopped, an outward sign of an inward state, or, in both cases, a non-sign of a non-state.

However, a year or so ago, my mother gave me a purse for my birthday. I was somewhat put out that she had not respected my purselessness. But the purse was small and of a new style—a quilted cloth purse with a spaghetti-string shoulder strap. The colors and pattern were beautiful—a dark green background with cabbage roses and lighter green leaves for the figures. It was light. It couldn't hold much except my slim billfold, a handkerchief, a pen or two. So I started carrying a purse again.

Reclaiming my purse is a way of reclaiming my value. There is power in the purse. If attacked, I could use it to defend myself. And its inner workings remain a sacred mystery for my husband, who never tries to find anything in my purse, but always brings it to me like a supplicant presenting a priestess with the holy of holies.

"MORE HERSELF THAN SHE IS"

Barbara A. Rouillard

*"The poet is representative. She stands among partial women for the
complete woman… The young woman reveres women of genius,
because, to speak truly, they are more herself than she is…
For all women live by truth and stand in need of expression."*
Emerson

before you
I went to bed early.
crisp, cotton sheets smoothed,
hem folded neatly
across my breasts.
two pillows plumped
beneath my head
and a face scrubbed clean—

                          pre-pubescent girl—

bed, body
all my own. but needing
the streetlight for comfort.
its gleaming brightness
hitting
the empty outer side
of my bed.

with you
the sheets
snap
from mattress corners.
one pillow, having fallen,
stays wedged
between bed and wall.
the quilt drapes your body
that lies atop mine.
another blanket
twisted, coiled
between our legs.

and in the blackness of my room,
shade pulled tightly down,
I smell a wood fire?
leather or flannel? you.
I fall to sleep.   or don't,   remembering,
George Sand did it.   then,
her bitter, ex-lover exclaimed her
a callous bitch—
claims
even after the most intimate evenings,
would awaken to find her
hunched at her desk,
clothed,
scribbling away
by the light of a candle.

and I believe him.
believe that's where
he would have found her.

before you
I liked to get up early.
take my coffee to my table.
wake to an open, fresh, clear mind.
mine. watch a sunrise,
hear the downshift
of early-morning
delivery trucks
pass my window as I worked.

now I taste
your toothpaste,
feel my skin rise.   my breasts,
the most sensitive
they have ever been.
travel the day
with the soreness
that reminds me
I chose
to stay longer
with you, not rising
until I had heard
a steady stream
of morning traffic.   but,

Sylvia Plath did it.   up at three a.m.,
before her children awakened,
spewed forth frantically
her *Ariel*
that winter.

still buying
that packaged
feminine mystique,
trying hard to ignore
this filthy apartment, wanting so badly,
but can't offer,
my most complete "woman."
not this artist
who lives with passion
and has to earn her own keep.   and remembering,

Elizabeth Barrett wanted only to read and write.
brilliant, pretty, eldest daughter
given Greek and Hebrew,
Latin, Portuguese... without ever leaving home.
never to be disturbed
with family tiptoeing by her room.   fame,
then Robert Browning
came.   yet,
Harriet Beecher Stowe
a year after
her seventh baby was born
wrote *Uncle Tom's Cabin*

and changed a world.

I want
forever
your life
to weave and wind
through mine.   but I fear
a rent
through the fibers
of this tapestry
I have woven so tightly
around me.

for a woman
in need of expression,

life is hard.

OKAY IN BERKELEY

Elaine Starkman

Last night I drove to Berkeley to hear
a poet. I liked her lines and
jotted them down. They weren't mine.

I went to her party.
My hair looked like hell,
but I was in Berkeley. I was invited.

I sat alone not with other guests
guests who drank wine. I drank tea.
It was okay not talking.

I ate chips by the fistful.
A young novelist I could be like
except I'm not so young and
don't do novels smiled at me.

On my way out, I waved to a Berkeley
big shot everyone knew but nobody outside
the room cared about. He sat alone,
eating chips by the fistful.

Winding out of the hills, my wheels sang:
       It's okay to meet novelists
  who write more and publish younger
  We all have ten sunshine minutes—
    before we fall out of fame—and nobody
cares—like all those people in Tibet or Ohio
and if this truth has taken me
twenty-years to learn
      that's okay too.

SMARTS

Stephanie Pall
(Submitted by Ellen Pall)

It's enough to make you wonder.
Christ, with his parables
Mohammed his Koran—
I mean, you think about it:
these people were not dummies
they were sharp cookies, all.
I guess Buddha could have had
just about anything he wanted
and all he wanted was a begging bowl,
a yellow robe and a few minutes of your time.

CHAPTER FOUR

GIFTS OF THE BODY-LANDS
THE INSTINCT TO TRUST THE GUT

The water is my blood and the earth is my bed.
From these simple things there is formed a web.
A web of wholeness and a creative force
that moves us beyond the course
of what we would have imagined
or planned with our lives.

$25 AN HOUR AT THE YMCA

Kathleen Moore

very Wednesday from 8–9 PM I lie on the narrow, flat massage table, my stomach and chest made comfortable by a foam pad under the flannel sheet. Sharon begins with my left leg. I have told her to add my arms and legs to the usual shoulders and back. It is my last hour with her and I want my whole body, at least as much of it as I dare let her touch, to feel her hands so I can impress this memory on every muscle so they will never forget her.

Most weeks she asks if I want my "tummy" done, a code word for that whole part of myself from breasts to thighs—this part of me that has lain protected by her flannel sheet from the first tentative half hour six months ago, when I must have been so tense and rigid I could have remained suspended in mid-air without the table under me. I have never answered yes to that question and she has never inquired further.

She must know how risky it has been for me to come here at all, to let her touch my neck and shoulders and back, my toes and fingertips. Certainly she knew when her fingers touched that muscle on the lower left side of my back, just above my waist. Each time it rippled as if touched by an electric shock and forced her hands to stop. "Don't touch me," that muscle screamed. After a month it began to relent, still giving that initial scream of fear. Then as her fingers paused, reassuring, it would give in and let her caress that frightened child muscle that held all the pain and confusion of forty-five years.

I remembered that electric ripple of terror, too ticklish to be painful but too painful to be funny, from a thousand years ago, the first time I made love. When he touched that spot, I felt for the briefest second as if he'd reached into my back and pierced that muscle with a hundred sharp pins. We laughed about it, but I asked him not to touch me there and he carefully avoided that small circle on my back. I didn't know then what it was anymore than I know now. But Sharon has brought it out of its lifetime of hiding, and given it the precious realization that it can be caressed and loved and healed.

Tonight, as usual, I have a headache. This will make it harder to concentrate on the feeling of her hands touching me, but I must focus all my attention on this so I can imagine it next Wednesday when she is gone, and I am lying instead in my bed with only my cat curled up at my side to comfort me. I am aware of her fingers making little circles on my ankles, on that soft indentation under the protruding round bone. She presses firmly on the bottom of my foot, pushing up on the arch so I am aware that it *is* an arch, that it is not flat. Her thumbs trace a thin line between the bones ending at each toe, pulling, releasing them from their cramped togetherness in my black leather, middle-aged career woman shoes. I become aware of every cell in that foot, each toe now becomes a sentient being, a friend. They should each have a name, I think. The first time this happened, I wanted her to spend the whole hour on just my feet, but the rest of my body was in so much need that I couldn't afford that luxury.

She covers my left leg and foot with the flannel sheet before uncovering the right leg. I feel chill but know that the motion of her hands over my skin, pressing into the nooks and crannies of my innermost body, will create sustaining warmth. I imagine that I am dead and have been laid on my funeral bier above the logs that are set ablaze. The flames do not hurt but warm me. They will burn through my flesh and release my soul from my no longer useful body and I will fly into freedom. By the time Sharon covers my right leg and moves to my arm, I am warm enough.

As she repeats the same strokes and pressures on my hands that she used on my feet, I become aware of the similarity between my arms and legs, my hands and feet, my fingers and toes. It is so obvious; I must always have known this! Yet it strikes me now as the most amazing insight. Of course, we used to be beings with four legs; all our limbs were the same. That race memory is so old, so faint. But Sharon's deep touching revives this mythic knowledge. These muscles and bones, now only distant cousins, remember that once they were brothers and sisters. The realization of this "physicalness," this "animalness," of my body is a wonder. This must be how a baby feels when she discovers her toes and puts them in her mouth, or begins to crawl, using arms and legs alike, four pieces of the self that act together, to balance the body, to give symmetry and completeness. I missed this body awareness as a child. My body was not allowed to move and play like other children's were. Mine was too often imprisoned in a bedroom, not much bigger than this massage room, stripped bare of all softness and texture. No rugs or curtains or blankets or stuffed animals. Bare wood floor, metallic Venetian blinds on the windows, a foam rubber pillow, plastic covering the mattress, bleached white sheets and pillowcase. Paper cut-out dolls to play with—flat, two-dimensional creatures that even my overly active imagination could never bring fully to life.

I lived in my mind, never in my body. My body only brought distress to me and those around me. It brought terror to my heart and fear in my mother's eyes when my lungs would not work well enough to keep the breath moving in and out with the constant regularity that others, without asthma, take for granted. I could never assume that the next breath would be there. I lived with a constant uncertainty about life. A chest so thin that each rib was singularly outlined against my skin, heaving in and out, putting forth a mighty effort to gasp the tiniest bit of air which was never enough and gasp again, desperate now for more before the first had time to flow completely in.

Even now, 40 years later, when I think of "my body," I think of my lungs wheezing like an ancient accordion struggling to play one more song but so weak that only faint, squeaky sharps and flats whisper from its tattered folds. Is it any wonder my shoulders and back still ache from that enormous effort to stay alive? How did that frail, tiny body do it? A champion weight-lifter could not put out more effort to lift his thousand-pound barbells than that tired little girl did to get one feeble breath.

Sharon gives me my body with her touch. She introduces me to those muscles that other children met when they were one or five or eight years old. "Here are your feet and ten toes."

I smile as she pulls on each one and say to myself, "This little piggy went to market..."

"Here are your legs," she teaches me. Not inert tree stumps, but living limbs that dance with the rhythms of the earth. "Here are your arms," that stretch to touch my farthest dreams, that held my baby surrounding him with protection and warmth. Here are my fingers that circle around this pen and write these words. Every muscle suddenly real, finally alive, naming itself, free after all the years of prison. Sharon has unlocked the cell door and led me out.

The hour has ended. The tape recorder clicked off, startling us both. But she turns the tape over and keeps on, because it is the last time, because she is leaving this city, going somewhere even she doesn't know yet, but going away. I can't bear the thought of this ending. Every week I waited for Wednesday the way other people wait for the weekend. Now Wednesdays will only bring a memory and a longing for that gentle touch that tamed me.

In Antoine de Saint Exupery's *The Little Prince,* a harried fox begs the prince to tame him. The prince must come to the same place at the same time every day. "First you will sit down at a little distance form me," the fox instructs the prince. "I shall look at you out of the corner of my eye, and you will say nothing... You will sit a little closer to me every day." When the fox has been tamed and the prince must leave, the fox weeps. The prince says that being tamed "has done you no good at all!" But the fox replies, "You see the grain fields down yonder? You have hair that is the color of gold. The grain, which is also golden, will bring me back the thought of you. And I shall love to listen to the wind in the wheat..."

I have come every week for six months at the same time and I have been tamed. The muscle that screamed in terror is now quiet; the right shoulder lies flat; my arms relax at my sides. Sharon has gone and I want to weep. But like the little prince, Sharon has golden hair; and like the fox, when I see wheat waving against a summer sky, it will bring me back the thought of her. My muscles and skin will remember and I shall love to listen to the wind in the wheat.

DEAR BODY

Janine Canan

Dear Body, gazing in the mirror it is you
that I behold with thankfulness.
You have been faithful these forty years.
With only a sore knee at puberty, some intestinal
rumblings before authority and teary outpourings
in the face of love, have you occasionally
asserted independence, disapproval, disregard of me.

Nor can I seriously object to the lines in your brow
that reveal where I have been thinking,
or to the downward curve of your mouth
that indicates grief I have carried since birth.
Your nose I thought too wide, has lengthened with time
that forces decision, and your white thighs
that frightened me, console me through darkening nights.

What good shoulders you have, I admit;
your soft breasts amaze me, and curving mortal hips.
When I see you naked so, still scarcely known,
I wonder, have I not served you well enough,
neglecting, depriving you of proper lovers—
the surging, languorous caress of bluegreen ocean,
the wild and powerfully exacting dance.

What a different story had I lived for you,
my devoted, solid, healthy Body,
with your hands of a potter or a surgeon,
strong enough to gather grain for a life of simple
satisfying eating. What patience you have shown
this lethargic, sedentary, moody being
who borrowed you, she claims, for higher reason.

Sitting waiting, while she thinks and dreams,
craving only quiet spaces, beauty in which
to lose herself on ever longer, more voluptuous
and deeper journeys, you must be a saint.

With your delicate, hyper-sensitive nerves—
painstakingly cultivated by erratic Mother Karma
who one moment forgets, the next grips violently,

so aware everything irritates or gives you
overwhelming pleasure, ecstatic wicked Body,
maniacally driven from one unreachable extreme
to another, isn't it obvious how, torn
between joy and terror, you became a poet,
passionately vibrating instrument, house
of the certain yet doubting, ever shifting eye.

Earthbody, brief spouse, what a strangely
inconvenient marriage. Yet you are my only
true support. And although you may never
fathom what I secretly am, may you—
who accepted the nature of existence itself—
stay with me, in your lovely halo of death,
till I depart, dearest Body, my slave, my queen.

ON DISTANCE

Patricia Kelly

Perhaps it would be better
to feel entirely unloved.

For there is always
this terrible distance.
This ash dusted inner distance,
like earth burned in retreat
from a fearful invader.

And the inner voices whispering
to remember the doors to Spirit
and imagination where thought
creates simply by being.

But I am in the flesh,
a thought's embrace wears thin
and harsh through years and distance;
the damning distance, like a beach
abandoned by the surf, a house
deserted in an echoing wood.

For I know, without ever having known,
the way a newborn infant knows to suckle,
that there is a loving to be yearned for.

A brief fingerwinding closeness
in which the blood web of our flesh
is woven gently together in a common pulse:
    where nothing is lost or lonely.
    and everything is gained,
    here, now, spiritflesh.
    no distance.

MY THIRTY YEARS WITH BREASTS

Melanie Hammer

1. How Do I Work These?

"Jump up and down," my mother says, frowning at me in the dressing room mirror. "No, that won't do. Here, try this bra. Now jump."

In the locker room before and after gym class, I look for any other girl whose breasts have grown as fast as mine, careful not to get caught peeking. Finally I find her. For days afterwards, while tying my sneakers or buttoning my dark blue gymsuit, I study her out of the corner of my eye to see how she carries them, if she stands up straight or hunches her shoulders, what her bras are like.

Eileen, a year behind me when I'm in eighth grade, is a quiet girl, so mousy, so frightened that she has to get up on stage. Somehow she convinces me to join her in a talent show. She comes by my house one afternoon with a stack of records and works us through a dance routine that she can carry off well and that I can follow.

After our first public rehearsal, she pulls me aside and tells me to wear a bra, that we look like a girlie show. I don't tell her that I am wearing a bra.

"Jump," my mother says, and shakes her head. She sorts through the bras in her hand. "Try this one."

I trace my finger around the hard, stiff molding of the cup, like armor. "What is this stuff?" I ask.

"Ah," she says, nodding, "underwire."

2. That Obscure Object of Desire

I grow older, I get strange urges. Some of them seem to be coming from my breasts. I learn to kiss, sometimes even guys I really like.

The summer I turn sixteen, I start going with Ace. In addition to a car and a driver's license, Ace has a boat. He teaches me to water ski, a feat I manage without losing either piece of my bathing suit.

Usually as we motor out of the harbor into the bay, I'm standing up, the better to drape myself over Ace and admire his blond hair, his square jaw, his blue eyes. One day he asks me if I'd noticed the guy on the day-sailer coming in as we were going out.

"He couldn't keep his eyes off you," Ace says. "He made me feel proud."

That night he asks me to go steady. I say yes. His ring is too big for my finger, but I happily string it on a chain around my neck, where it perches above my breasts.

It's more fun to kiss Ace than anyone before him. I believe I've fallen in love. The longer we go together, the more I think there might be other things we could do besides kissing. One hot summer night I'm wearing a scooped-neck tank top and we're making out. Ace starts kissing my neck and goes lower and lower until he reaches the tops of my breasts. I can't wait to see what's going to happen next; I'm practically holding my breath. He stops.

"I'm sorry," he says later. "I know you're not that kind of girl."

"That's all right," I say, but I'm busy decoding. Ace obviously admires my breasts and wants to touch them. I want him to, but apparently I shouldn't. We break up before I crack the code.

One day we have plans for Ace to take me shopping with a couple of friends, but I get an asthma attack and have to stay home. Sweet guy that he is, Ace takes my friends to the mall anyway. Later Deedee calls me up and tells me Marlene made them walk through lingerie where she mentioned to Ace that her breasts were bigger than mine.

"How can she be that ridiculous," I say. "Hers just look big because she's short."

Ace and Marlene get married after high school.

The first time Danny comes to pick me up, he has his brother's 240Z. After that he comes for me in his mother's Dart, which has a comfortable back seat where my breasts and I can go for a spin. He doesn't worry about what kind of girl I am and he clearly doesn't want to fall in love or go steady or anything like that. My breasts and I begin our adventures.

3. And They Grew and They Grew

"Try this one," my mother says, holding out a white bra. "This is a Flower Bali with underwire and four hooks. I bet this will do the trick."

My breasts have a life of their own. Every four weeks they get achy and only consent to be squeezed into certain bras, something else I have to remember when I get dressed in the morning. The floppy flannel shirts and jeans of the late sixties allow a margin for error. But only in winter. Springtime brings halter tops, tube tops, semi-sheer India prints. Women go braless. This looks fabulous on people fortunate enough to have perky breasts that stand on their own. In my case bralessness would involve letting them dangle to my waist, something for which the world and I are not yet prepared. I spend the entire '60s bra'd, except, of course, for skinnydipping on darkest summer nights.

When I go off to college, I gain weight. My breasts, in true go-with-the-flow fashion, gain weight, too. I have all the bras that get too small in the back of my top drawer.

As we get larger, my breasts attract more attention. I understand this attention has nothing to do with me personally, and I experiment with different ways of handling it.

One afternoon I'm admiring shoes on Fifth Avenue. A voice behind me says, "Hey, you have big tits."

I turn around and find myself eye level with a thin dark man. I look him up and down. "Yeah?" I say. "Well, I bet your dick's too small for you to do anything about it."

He's speechless long enough for me to get away.

4.   The Container of the Uncontainable

A list of things I could wear if I had my breasts done: Speedo tank suits, bathing suits with shelf bras or hardly any support, racerback tank tops and bras, narrow ribbed sweaters, the next wedding I was asked to be in, I could actually do it in a strapless dress. Underwire would vanish from my life.

At a party my friend Jane wears a midnight blue strapless velvet dress with one of those shirred elastic bodices that clings from the tops of her breasts to her hips, where the skirt of the dress flares out. I know that under it she wears a strapless bra for a little support, but her shoulders flow out from the dress, pale and smooth, unmarked by bra-strap grooves.

What I would lose: after the doctor's cut and scooped, my breasts would look prettier, assuming they've been sewn back on straight, but they wouldn't feel as much because of nerve damage. We may have our disagreements, but my breasts are also a source of pleasure. Sometimes they know we're having a good time before I do, and the nipples stand up and salute themselves, telling me to pay attention. My breasts know more than I do about joy.

"Forty DD," my mother says, looking at me in the dressing room mirror. "Wow."

"That's only because I'm pregnant," I snap. "They're not going to be this big forever."

"Ha," she says, but when she sees my expression, she adds, "Well, maybe. I've gone up a size every decade since I was twenty, but maybe you won't."

5.   Rapprochement

As the pregnancy progresses, my breasts get bigger. They ask for their own bed, their own car to ride in. Then my belly swells up and for once in my life, my breasts don't look so large anymore. They decorate themselves as if for a party, changing color, growing darker, threaded with purple veins that criss-cross like rivers on a map to a secret place they've been without me.

I sit in the birthing room with my newborn daughter. All the books say I won't have milk for seventy-two hours and not to worry. The books all say that the sucking instinct is a powerful, natural one, implying that I shouldn't worry. I look at my daughter and see that her head is smaller than my breast. In fact, as I study her, I decide that her whole body is smaller than my breast.

Only half an hour old, she latches right on and sucks. I give her five minutes a side, just like the books say, and she falls asleep. According to all those books, she has just taken colostrum, the protein breasts manufacture for babies right after birth. But without having seen it, how can I believe it?

I look at my breasts as if I could see inside them with x-ray eyes. Then, my daughter cradled in one arm, I press gently around one nipple. A drop of pure gold comes out.

What do you know? These things actually work!

When the baby gets older and stops nursing my breasts start to shrink a little, and each time I can get into a smaller bra I throw out the larger ones. At the back of my drawer are bras I've held onto for years, the ones I aspire to, with hooks in the front or just a couple in the back, the ones in colors other than white, beige and black. I wear Flower Balis while I wait.

Meanwhile my breasts have turned dangerous. I'm from an ethnic group that's "prone," I have a certain amount of body fat, and there are people in my family who have had variations. On the other hand, I nursed my kids and have a relatively low-fat diet. I hate to view them with suspicion, but it seems my breasts have to be watched.

I know what to expect at a mammogram, but I don't quite believe it until I see each breast squeezed flatter than breast pancake between clear glass plates. For the first time in our lives together, I feel sorry for them.

I'm one of the few women I know who likes to shop for bathing suits, but bra shopping has always been a soulless chore. Year after year, bra designers reaffirm their beliefs that boobs like mine belong to old ladies who want to stuff their breasts into the primmest asexual white or beige.

Then one day, my friend Lilys says, "Guess what? I just landed a project to redesign the packaging for Bali bras. Do you know they haven't changed the basic design of their Flower Bali bra for forty years?" I know, I can vouch for a number of those years personally.

When I go down another bra size, I go shopping. Suddenly the whole world has gone to color, and I can't tell which bras are my size by just looking from a distance. Flowers, paisleys, racerbacks, front hooks—they're all suddenly coming up in my size. Where before, my breasts and I never had anything to wear when we wanted to go out and play, I can now have a well-dressed breast. We try them all on, admire ourselves in the mirror, and know we can go anywhere we please. My breasts have finally made it!

BULIMIA

Lisa Alvarado

Before you take the laxatives
sacred manna of escape
you know it is fear
that eats your entrails

Vomiting up
years of anger
Anger wrapped in dough
Sugar coated
You struggle
to get rid
of what will make you
big
In smallness there must
be relief
Relief from the anger
that sears your soul

You run from bathroom
to bathroom
In a panic
to put out the fire
A moment's delay
and you'll burst
into flames.

DAMN IT, CALL ME BEAUTIFUL

Lois Barth

 was brought into this world through a woman, a woman who was informed daily how plain she was, that she had buck teeth, thick legs, and that the big breasts that hung on her smaller frame were something to hide, to be ashamed of. In a sweltering room with no ventilation on a hot August day, she lay crying on her bed when the only summer apparel available for her was a pink gingham halter. She ate the red pulp of blood oranges for she heard they were poisonous and would cause her to die instantly. It was a wives' tale, and unfortunately her death was of a slower nature; her soul withered, a flower with no chance to bloom.

She vowed, "It will be different for my kids." They will feel wanted and the girls will feel beautiful, like the precious porcelain doll that watched from her wooden hutch.

I was born. A joyous bundle of child mass, cookie dough face with brown saucer eyes. She beamed, "Just like your father, you're beautiful." I actually look like her. When anyone comments on our resemblance, she shrugs, "Oh, thank you, I wish I looked like her, actually she looks just like her father, he's the one with the looks in the family."

Damaged children become damaged adults by continuing the legacy or by doing the opposite. "Honey, you're beautiful," over and over. Like a wound that was not exposed to the open air to heal, it became transplanted under my skin. "You're beautiful, everyone's looking at you."

I grew up spending hours in front of the mirror looking at me, scrutinizing my rounded hips, full breasts, naturally pinched-in waist, strong-angled, full, broad features, remnants of my third-generation Eastern European roots.

"You're beautiful." I never felt it. Only in brief moments when no one was home, and I slipped into my mother's white stiletto heels, floral push-up bra and danced in front of the mirrored wall that lined my living room. And when I danced, I was at home. I flew to places I seldom visited on the earthly plane. In those few select moments I felt beautiful.

But those moments passed and I went back to the world confused. There were no boys lined up pining for my affection. I would not be elected prom queen or be the model in the magazines. I would never be called beautiful—ethnic, attractive, sensual, even striking, perhaps, but not beautiful.

Like a fleeting bird that once in a lifetime jumps on your hand, but takes flight if you try to catch it, I know beauty is an ephemeral thing. Although I refuse to define myself through society's limited aesthetic scope and am more connected to my essence, my pain, my joy, I wrestle with that part of me that still cries out, "Damn it, call me beautiful."

The years pass and with every tear that flows into the river of my being, a stream forms that bridges me back to myself. I am finally walking into the person I am meant to be, at home in my skin. I look in the mirror. My face says it all. There is life in my eyes, and simple little crevices around my mouth from the delicious bounty of laughing feasts I have fed upon. My lips are full from all the words spared and not, the frozen smiles I gave so no one would see how scared I was.

Life exists in my face, the years lost, the years promised, the years lived. There is the soft skin, slightly softer as I carry on in my years, the child-woman face under the glare of the harsh bathroom light, the dim circles under my eyes from the tumultuous night's sleep and the morning's crusty edge. Youth and wisdom live simultaneously.

In so many ways I look more like myself than ever before. I've settled into my features, my tears have washed the pain of yesteryear into the fountain called experience. At times I feel beautiful.

AGING VENUS

Altha Edgren

His offertories were this plate of blood oranges,
kiwi and bitter chocolate,
strawberries dipped in cream,
flutes of sparkling cider.

Blue columned sconces dripped candlelight,
before a card depicting "The Awakening of Adonis."
The incense of their scents mingled,
salt, musk and vanilla lace with hymns of gypsy violins.

Before entering the temple
he sang praises to her middle-aged body,
massaged jasmine and rose oil into her feet,
whispered a testament of poems by Baudelaire.

"You have the body of a twenty-year-old," he said,
and she wondered,
could he not see the dimpled folds of skin
left over from where the babies grew,
breasts shrunken from nursing, and
the scar along the ribline where the knife
entered to remove the sac of crystalline gall.

She thought to ask him,
but his eyes were already closed,
his head already bowed,
his body already arced
in the wordless ecstasy of worship.

CRESCENT MOON

Roseann Lloyd
for Cheryl Bates

Her hands are gentle, smooth, the tension is
dissipating, being drawn
away. I pull back from the pain I know
is leaving my right eye. My shoulders groan
when she works them. I let my mind

pass through images and words: go *away, old dog
of the body*. It's so quiet in the room
we can hear the wind in the elms, the geese
in the park. They're honking wildly
flapping. So noisy, they must be mating.

My arms are light and graceful, my hands
receivers of pleasure, not just tools
for work. There's some desire
to cry
about this pleasure.

I'm in my own thoughts.
Cheryl says, "The new moon!"
"Oh," I say, coming back to her presence
vaguely, "is there a new moon today?"

"No," she says, "I'm talking about the moon
on you. Here.
The mark
of the Goddess."

I laugh out loud. Nobody has ever
called my scar a moon.
The raised crescent
across my round bottom.
It's been there so long, over forty years.

A first memory from when I was three, my first
defiance of my mother.
I had to take baths in the kitchen sink
because I refused to take a shower.
Mother put a flat plug in the sink, an empty
mayonnaise jar on top of the plug
to hold it in place.

She told me to sit still.
I didn't want to sit still. I wanted
to swim and dive, to climb up high
like the women in the summer at the city pool.
I made it to the top of the jar.
I balanced, reached my arms to the sky,
naked and slippery as a silvery fish.
You can imagine the rest.

They came running with bedsheets,
there was so much blood.
The glass in the water
was glistening
in crescent-shaped shards.
They threw me in the middle of the sheets, naked,
like Dumbo, falling
down into the firemen's net.

What's funny is
I don't remember the pain. I remember
the anticipation
of climbing, the thrill of the
risk, just before
the dive.

        I don't remember the pain, I
remember contemplating, in that split
second, yes, contemplating
the nature of flying, the welcome
of the waters below.

I remember the lapping of
the waters, the shimmer of the moons,
me, moving, relaxed
and graceful.

And it is this moment
I know as the true claim
of the Goddess: *pain recedes
away from us, delight
remains.*

*(Note: "Send away old dog of the body," is from "A Summer
Prayer" by John Brandi.)*

CHAPTER FIVE

GIFTS OF ADVERSITY
GRIEF AND GRACE

When I was a little girl I dreamed that my mother died.
Deeply upset, I stood back from the dream
to see that we all lived on a great big tree,
and my mother just went to live on another branch.
So even though I couldn't see, hear or touch her,
we were still a part of the same big tree.

BECOMING A WRITER

Roseann Lloyd
my brother the artist dead of an overdose at age 21

They opened the earth and put him in
his gravestone a slab on my heart my voice box
bolted shut

desperate to get death off my chest
the dreaded thought *the end of our family*
I followed him into the grave

took notes
there was no stopping it once it started
the rush of feelings the flow

of words the insistent
search for truth the pleasure
of the black ink pen in my hands

family secrets spilled out of me
like so many missing socks
I no longer needed to mate

my brother reached out his hand
raised me up from the shabby couch
smiled his bad-boy rabbi smile

there's an empty place at the family table
the artist's place you sit there
you might as well enjoy it

grass grew around his grave
I walked out into it
it was soft and green and tempting under my feet

the meadow had a yellow aura
Brother I said my voice
riding my breath with ease

Oh loosened tongue
Oh naked feet
Oh grave that is a door

THE SOLACE OF THE WEE OF LIFE

Myrtle Archer

"W hen life gets almost too tough to bear..." the neighbor patted my shoulder as coffee-cup-tension clenched my whole body and mind, "...I turn to the wee of life. I find that's a Grand Canyon in help. So many heartaches in life we can do nothing about but accept them... and once I'm certain of that, I turn to the wee of life—for comfort, when all else fails."

I stared at her. How could I spare a thought for the wee of life with the grief and anguish in my heart for my aged father-in-law who shot my aged mother-in-law, an Alzheimer's victim, and then shot himself? Why couldn't my husband and I have prevented such a tragedy? Why hadn't we foreseen the old gentleman's intent when he'd said over and over, "Mama and I have lived too long." But... too late for self-flagellation. All that was left to me was to learn to cope with the painful days that loomed ahead. Life whacked out so many situations—most much smaller than this one—which tortured, but which were beyond any human's ability to act to change the situation itself.

"I'll try anything that might help lift this weight of grief and recrimination from me," I said to the neighbor. "In situations when I can't do anything to help, I usually scrub walls. But I've already done that. Scrubbing walls is therapeutic for situations of lesser anguish."

"Is that why you have such marvelously clean walls?" She laughed after her words, and I tried to laugh with her.

The funerals were over. I'd written the thank-you notes for the deluge of kindness, attended to the most urgent tasks at my in-laws house. I'd taken what comfort I could from religion. The days stumbled by in a fog of work, grief, anguish, and attempts to comfort my husband. "Time will sweep you away from all this to a better day," I repeated to him and he nodded numbly.

But I required something more at hand than time. "The wee of life," I repeated to myself. "The wee."

In sunshine I studied a small design of lawn, a flowerbed of scarlet zinnias, the sweep of cloudless blue sky. Full-blown golden chrysanthemums hurt me with their beauty, which my in-laws would never see again. My fog did not lift. Studying the wide world had been therapeutic for some sorrows and troubles, but for this one I must go smaller than that—smaller. Maybe I'd have to resort to a microscope and study the—to me—unseen.

I studied an ant exploring a green geranium leaf, one of a host of apples reddening on a tree—how perfect the apple was, how poignant its blush of red, how beautiful its curves.

A blade of grass braved a crack between driveway and fence. A line traced up the center of the green sword of the blade in faultless symmetry. I contemplated the heart of one pink overblown rose on a rose bush. Perfect stamens centered it. With the images of four of the wee of life in my mind, I turned back toward the house and sought comfort from the images.

Gradually and deliberately I studied more and more of the wee of life: the perfection and fragility of a newborn baby's tiny fingernails, the pureness of vision through a just-cleaned window pane, the roughness of an old tree trunk, the silk of hair on a white cat's ear, a sow bug curling into a brown corrugated ball, the veining on a small white and black rock, the sinuous look of a child's sweet and vulnerable neck, intricate wrinkles on the back of an old man's neck, the crimson dance of flame on a log in a fireplace, the geometric pattern of seeds in a sliced tomato, a trickle of pellucid water down a camellia leaf, the chirp of a cricket, the ruffle of a petal of a purple pansy, the flick of a lizard's tongue, the whisper of a breeze, the mosaic of earliest fall leaves on the ground.

The symmetry of one cloverleaf entranced me as did a grain of salt in purest white on the yolk of my breakfast egg. Telephone wires made an ugly maze in the whole, but just one small intersection of them made an interesting pattern against the sky and the masterpiece of one curving petal of a bronze chrysanthemum parried all other thoughts. Wonder pierced me with sweet pain as I realized how the wee I saw was all lovely in all their individual ways.

Gradually I shifted my mind from the wee to the larger. I contemplated the whole rose bush without anguish, studied the sweep of sky and clouds. Then adrift in the sense of the wonder of life, acceptance crept in.

When my neighbor stepped over on her daily visit, I said, "You were right. The wee of life has been a tremendous help to me in getting me over the hurdles of this. Even in the midst of trouble, the world in tiny spots is a wonderful, beautiful and serene place. And it was still here, waiting to comfort me."

Now when heartaches come, as they come so often in life, first I try to do all I can to alleviate them. But after that, for comfort and solace I turn to the wee of life.

The more painful the heartache, the smaller I, for a time, focus my gaze.

THE BRIGHT CLOTH

Kate Barnes

A child of seven
comes home from school
and her mother
(who is mad)
chases her
around the table
with a long, sharp
pair of scissors.

Better not to say
what games her father
used to play with her
up in her bedroom
before he left.
At least he spoke to her
kindly, and sang to her
about twinkling stars.

At night, alone,
she goes to sleep
with her stuffed bear clutched
across her chest.
"If someone stabbed me
while I was sleeping,
my friend would save me..."
and so she invents

safety from wishes,
love from the longing
of the heart in her thin
ribcage that has
to imagine affections
all around it,
in a silent toy,
in a cold star.

And she will grow up
still reaching outward
as if heaven
were in every drop
of hanging dew,
as if love
were in every grass blade—
everywhere!—

As if her strong soul
could stay warm
forever just by
wrapping itself
in the bright cloth
it keeps on weaving
from darkness
and the blind wind.

BREAKING THE SILENCE

R.H. Douglas

ear Diary...

My husband wants to make love. He is caressing me. His hands move down my thighs. He is kissing me between my legs, tender and compassionate. He is enjoying himself. It is only 5:00 a.m. and the lights are on. Usually we turn the lights off, but this morning we have been talking about long ago, childhood and growing up in the West Indies and about my mother, Miss Micey and Mr. Rudin, the man whose hand crawled up inside of me while I slept on the floor on bedding of old clothes next to the bed on which he slept with my mother. I was telling my husband about Mr. Rudin while I sat up in bed sipping coffee that my husband brought me. Now he wants to make love. I don't want to but I want to please him. I want to say *Yes, let's,* but a part of me is pulling back, pulling away, wanting him to stop touching me, stop molesting me. I feel tight inside. *Leave me alone.* But it is not fair to him, I think, he is my husband.

I try to put into words what I feel as his hands roam over me. I begin to see Mr. Rudin's hands and realize how my husband's big, strong black hands remind me of Mr. Rudin's. I now realize why I, a lover of mornings—as a married woman, hate the morning. I remember not only the image but also the emotion of being startled awake by Mr. Rudin's fingers firmly planted in my vagina. I cringe when I feel my husband's hands, but I never knew why, always pushing the feeling aside, believing something was wrong with me that I could not enjoy sex.

Seeing, feeling and identifying, I want to tell my husband this as he enjoys himself between my legs, but I am numb. How can I tell him this in the midst of his heat? Because he is my husband, I remain silent, succumb to his need and give him his pleasure even though it leaves me sad and angry.

Unlike my husband who wants to stir me awake, Mr. Rudin only operated when he believed me to be asleep. Whenever I stirred, Mr. Rudin's finger came to a standstill. Sometimes I laid awake, not stirring. He'd think I was sleeping and I'd feel his finger moving in me. Sometimes I pretended I was dreaming and not really feeling it. I didn't know I could pull his hand away or roll my body away or just tell him to stop. I had no words, no action, only the stillness of silence before the morning dawn.

Sometimes I wondered if it was okay for Mr. Rudin to do this to me. It seemed okay because when he moved his fingers there was a sweet feeling but it hurt too. I am not sure. I am not sure what I am feeling now.

My husband's tongue tickles my thighs. My husband's tongue brings me a tingling of pleasure. I feel his breath warm against the hairy softness around my vagina. My husband tongues my legs again and I look down at him, look down at myself in such a position. How vulgar, I think. How vulgar. Quickly I must shut that voice up and focus on enjoying my husband fondling and caressing me—trying so hard to bring me pleasure.

My legs, my legs don't look like mine! These are my mother's legs, spread wide open like a whore; and that is not my husband; that is one of my mother's men between her legs. This is not me, in this position. It could not be me. I wouldn't be in a position like this and acting as if I wanted to enjoy this feeling.

But I want to, if only I could let myself go, and forget Mr. Rudin's early morning hand, my alarm clock, before he got up to tend his fish-pots. No. I wouldn't get pleasure from this! Such a nasty act! But my husband obviously is. How disgusting to hear his grunts of satisfaction. What is my husband doing there? Why is he enjoying this nastiness? My God! I am going to crack up! This is not my husband. I am not like that! "Help me, help me," I scream, "don't let me be like that."

Startled, my husband looks up and comes to meet my face. He hugs me trying to understand what is happening. Why my sudden outburst in the midst of his pleasure. I see fear and concern in his eyes as I scream and thrash, flinging pillows and bed-sheets everywhere. I feel fear in my heart, real fear. Why am I acting like this? What is happening to me? I already dealt with this in therapy. I wrote about it in the Diary. Why now, again? Why now when I am trying to own my sexuality, my sensuality, without labeling myself *bitch*.

I thought I had it all together and had crossed this Mr. Rudin and being a whore like my mother Micey. But now I want to puke. My husband is struggling to hold me. I fight him with all my might and continue to scream, "I don't want to be like that! Help me please! Don't let me be like that!"

Suddenly he releases me and locks the door so the children are not awakened by my screams. He comes back, bewildered, his eyes saying, *God I hope she is okay...* He holds me, comforting, gently saying, "I love you, I love you, I love you." I hear him say it but I don't believe him. I don't trust who he is, he's not my husband. He is a man like Mr. Rudin, like another of my mother's men trying to molest me, trying to put his hands between my legs.

"Don't let them, don't let them touch me," I scream holding my legs together. "They're not touching you," he calmly says. "I can feel them. My vagina feels funny. It hurts, I can feel them. Don't let them touch me there, please." I plead with him to protect me from them, to keep them away; but he cannot. I can still feel their hands and the uncertain sensation causing pain and forced pleasure between my legs.

I don't own it anymore. It feels foreign. My legs tingle and my vagina is alive and warm. I scream louder as I feel myself losing breath. "I am choking. Don't let them put it in my mouth," I plead with him as I choke on the invisible penis. Suddenly I shoot straight up in bed. I am alive. But in an instant I know I will die if I do not break through this feeling. My voice is a hoarse whisper. I whimper like a cat kicked into a dark corner. I reach for a pillow and place it on my bare bottom and lay very still. I know it's okay now. My husband is looking at me, puzzled. I feel badly that he did not have his chance at an orgasm. I know he understands. But for how long? He will want to have sex again, and then what?

I know what's happening, I tell myself. And maybe now that I know, I can control it. I have always crawled out of my body when it's time for sex. I am never consciously present, only in fantasy. But this time I wanted to be brave and embrace the pleasure of the act. And I got caught with the light on; emotions flooding back like spasms of orgasms.

I dared believe it was water under the bridge. I thought it okay to lay back, observing and enjoying the action. Let myself be turned on without this inner fight; without going against the flow of my sexuality; without turning my mind off before letting myself be turned on. This time my mind did not turn off and I was beginning to take pleasure in the act.

I may never forget the sensation of sex as nastiness, nor the sound of my mother's whimpering like a cornered animal, too drunk most times even to enjoy herself. These memories may come back to haunt me but they will not prevent my growth, my healing, my welcoming myself into this life.

I hear the little girl scream, "How dare you? How dare you?" The little girl that felt betrayed, bruised, and hurt as the woman gave herself permission to enjoy the pleasure, to be turned on so boldly without exiting the body. "It's okay, I am a woman now," I want to tell her gently.

"Help me," I whimper and curl up to sleep exhausted. After a few minutes I feel my husband's hands still wanting to explore me. I thought he understood. How odd he can still enjoy sex with me after all this emotional stuff. I am not sure if I want to, if I should. I am a grown woman and I am still not sure.

I guess it is my duty to please him, not wanting to be called a cold woman, a woman not keen to his needs and therefore not a good wife. So sadly I say okay, giving in with my body before exiting; wanting to believe that by saying okay—by having sex, I will overcome the memories and be present while enjoying the act. Maybe, some day...

For now I see myself depart as I allow him his pleasure. I return after his moaning and groaning have died down. Only then, do I know it is safe to enter my body again, to claim my space inside myself and not be afraid of the pleasure reaching me and tempting me to enjoy!

HYSTERECTOMY

Sharon L. Charde

Listen. I have two stories to tell you. One will be expected, the other will be surprising. The first: "Mrs. Charde, your PAP smear came back Class II for the second time. We'd better schedule a colposcopy to look at the cervix more carefully." "Mrs. Charde, you'll need a cone biopsy, the PAP is still Class III." "Mrs. Charde, you must have a hysterectomy."

I had cervical intraepithelial neoplasia, abnormal cells in the cervix. I had the second and third opinions, consultations with Nora Coffey of HERS Foundation (Hysterectomy Educational Resources and Materials) that advised restraint, test rereading, explored the possible presence of HPV virus. I had confrontations with glib physicians who insisted that my uterus was unneeded because of my age. I asked one of them how he'd feel if a professional suggested he have his testes removed since he really didn't need them, having had all the children he wanted. He looked down at his Weejuns and laughed nervously.

I got tired of telling the story of my cervix: the process of deciding what to do felt like another job. I made lists of pros and cons. I read Tarot cards, asked my dreams for messages, took beta carotene capsules and ate carrots. I thought about how my life could be devastated by the sentence, "Mrs. Charde, you have cancer." I bought a boogie board. I had an endocervical scraping after conflicting lab results. I had a letter from a Columbia expert telling my doctor that, in fact, I did have CIN III hidden in little pockets in my hacked-up cervix. It resisted excision, even after all the cuts. It would most certainly progress to cancer without a hysterectomy.

Finally I knew I had to go under the knife. I was scared. I stayed in the purity of terror for awhile, but slowly became less ambivalent. I had fought to save my children's first home, wanting my body to walk into old age as complete as it had been in my youth. It seemed I had lost the fight—or so I thought.

And here's the second story: I scheduled the surgery two weeks before Christmas, reasoning the holiday would be a good time to be away from my work as a psychotherapist, and also that it would keep me absent from the relentless seasonal cheer I have found painful since my younger son died seven years ago. I packed my bag with poetry books and a heart-shaped rock from the Block Island beach, and decided on an epidural anesthetic since this would contribute to a quicker recovery, although it would keep me awake for the operation.

I told my husband and son I needed lots of their love. I laughed in the operating room.

That's where the second story really begins: an opening cut through fascia, ligaments, blood, muscle and nerves to lift out the mother-organ, created a new space. I lost the monthly memory of mothering but I never thought I'd gain something else. Hands held on a hospital bed, feet rubbed on my linen living room couch, seven days worth of soup and bread in a wicker basket brought to my door—they healed me with their kindness. I was the giver given to. It was not without pain, tubes running in and out of my body, black loneliness in a dark hospital night, a thick red scar. But this opening cut receptivity into a tough independent woman. Friends old and new, husband, son, family marched in and claimed the space it created. They mothered me. I sat among gifts of yellow roses, a Christmas tree strung with red chili lights, snow falling—and I received.

Months later I carry still this unexpected softening. I mourn a loss, but never expected flowers to bloom in its place. Women, I have never felt better.

"PLAY FOR ME" –
A MOTHER'S BENEDICTION

Joey Kay Wauters

hear it as a prayer now, my mother's final words to me. I hear the words even though they were never spoken aloud, for my mother could no longer talk then. My husband and I sat by her hospital bedside, Mom smiling as she outwitted us with triple word scores on the Scrabble board in front of her. Scrabble was always a favorite family game, but in Mom's last days, it was more than just play; it was one of her few remaining forms of communication. Her tongue muscles weakened by Lou Gehrig's disease, Mom could no longer articulate words. Yet her crippled hands could still push the letters on the board to form words. After even that effort became too great for her, she painstakingly punched in some letters on her handheld computer. Her message to me was printed out on a thin ribbon of paper: "Play for me." She wanted us to continue the game without her.

I pushed aside the game, holding her hand in mine, telling her we would finish later. I didn't realize she had less than an hour left to live.

Losing a beloved parent is always a trial by fire for a daughter or son, especially when it involves a long terminal illness. And few illnesses match the devastation of Lou Gehrig's disease, known officially as amyotrophic lateral sclerosis (ALS). Doctors know neither the cause nor the cure for this progressive neuromuscular disease, which gradually causes all the motor nerves to die, resulting in paralysis of body parts and finally death when the victim can no longer talk, eat or breathe. Yet while the muscles atrophy and physical functions disintegrate, the mind is not affected at all, so patients are mentally aware that they are trapped in the now-useless shells of their bodies.

The specter of wasting away would be horrifying to anyone, but it is doubly cruel for athletes, hence the association with Lou Gehrig, the baseball player struck down in his prime in the 1930s. In my own family, the tragic irony was that my mother had been the healthiest and most physically fit of any of us. Although in her early seventies when diagnosed, she was still an avid backpacker and skier who danced weekly to rock music at the local disco with my father.

Mom's neurologist predicted that she would walk until the last week of her life, and she proved him right by not only walking but dancing up until her final days. The doctor believes it was due to her extraordinary physical conditioning that her legs continued to function even as her other muscles atrophied. Unlike most ALS patients, my mother was never confined to a wheelchair during the two years of her illness. In fact, upon hearing of my mother's death, one of her friends gasped, "Helen? She can't be dead. I just saw her at the disco two weeks ago!"

That life-embracing spirit is the legacy my mother left me. Mom was always a nature lover, introducing my two brothers and me at an early age to the joys of wildflowers and forest trails during summers at our family cabin in the Sierra Nevada mountains of California. While other girls sewed or went shopping with their mothers, mine took me backpacking and mountain climbing.

In her fifties, with her children grown and gone, she continued to pursue wilderness sports with such vigor that she became a local legend. At first she was a participant on Sierra Club backpacking ventures ranging from overnight trips to a wilderness trek of several weeks in Nepal. She was the oldest woman in Northern California to earn the Sierra Club's "gorge scrambling" badge, an honor bestowed on intrepid hikers who scramble along crumbling cliffs and wade through treacherous river gorges where no trails exist. Soon she became qualified as a Sierra Club leader herself, and in addition to leading weekend hikes, she formed her own mid-week hiking group. She was renowned for leading her flock on adventurous cross-country jaunts, one of which resulted in the discovery of a small, unnamed jewel of a lake that her fellow hikers dubbed "Helen's Lake." In her sixties, Mom tackled cross-country skiing, becoming proficient enough to whiz in and out of the snow-covered roads to our Sierra cabin.

Hardiness in adversity was her trademark. Once after hiking into a canyon alone she broke her arm when a boulder fell on her. She hiked out ten miles in pain, her badly fractured arm dangling by her side. On a week-long backpacking trip, she slipped and fell headfirst on a rocky trail, breaking her nose. Bandaged, she hiked two more days to complete the trip. These accidents caused her to increase her first-aid skills, but they did not stop her. She was back at her training regimen as soon as the doctors permitted, marching along country roads with a backpack full of bricks to stay in shape.

My mother's strength was spiritual as well as physical, as we witnessed when she was diagnosed with ALS in the spring of 1992. My father, a retired doctor who understood all too well the implications of this disease, sobbed as he phoned my husband Jim and me long distance to tell us. We broke down, too. But Mom shed no tears for herself, saying, "I've had a good long run. I've had a wonderful marriage, I enjoyed raising you children, and I've trekked all over the world. I'm grateful that I've lived my life to the fullest."

She continued to do so. Never bemoaning what she could not do, she sought new ways to pursue her passions. That summer, since she could no longer accompany Jim and me on our annual backpacking trip, we chose a guided llama trip instead so that she would not have to carry a pack. Later after camping on the ground became impossible, we took day hikes. And when hiking finally wearied her too much, Mom turned to an exercise bicycle to keep her legs in shape for her most beloved sport of all: dancing.

Since my father was not a hiker, dancing was the activity they shared throughout their fifty-year marriage. From the Big Band tunes of the '40s to disco of the '90s, they gyrated on the floor like partners decades younger. While the ALS slowed her down from their usual frenetic pace, Mom never gave up dancing, as it was an intrinsic part of the passionate love she and my father enjoyed. They continued to make regular treks to the disco even in the final months, to the astonishment of all.

Despite Mom's determined spirit, the weakness in her upper body took its toll. By August 1993 she could no longer eat or drink enough to sustain herself due to swallowing problems, and a gastric tube was inserted. Three times a day my father fed her through the tube at home, and she gradually gained enough strength to resume walking and dancing.

Mom had been the caretaker herself for so long that it was hard to have the tables turned on her. Her hands became extremely weak and she needed assistance with simple tasks such as washing or dressing herself. My father devoted himself to her care full-time, and my brothers and I visited as often as possible. Every time Mom and I went for a walk, I put on and took off her shoes. Almost every time she apologized for needing the help. "Don't worry, Mom," I said. "Just remember all the years you helped me with my shoes." My voice was light, but often I had to brush aside my tears as I tied her laces. I tried to be as brave as she was, but I felt helpless as I watched my vigorous mother deteriorate, muscle by muscle.

Even under such circumstances, Mom never despaired or lost her enjoyment of the miracles of the moment. A bird's song, a blue sky, a good book or a warm hug—such pleasures sustained her despite physical setbacks, and she took part in their wonder as fully as a child. I saw the beauty and abundance of the earth with new eyes, the eyes of the woman who had given me life and who saw life taken away from her without self-pity.

I couldn't help asking myself if my mother's calm acceptance of her fate was a façade she put on to keep us from grieving more than we already did. My father wondered, too. Once when I was visiting, he asked her in an anguished tone, "Honey, did you ever hide your tears from me? Do you ever sob into your pillow at night when I am asleep?" Mom looked at us with a wan smile and shook her head in a definite no. Neither of us could doubt the sincerity shining in her eyes. Yet it was no conventional sense of religion that comforted Mom; her spirituality derived from her intimate bond with nature and its seasons. Many times she and I climbed the mountains together to meditate on the setting sun. She was too close to the earth not to realize that the cycle of life encompassed death. And hers was near.

That final day I sat with her was one year ago now. Aspiration pneumonia was the stroke that felled her suddenly. A common result of ALS problems, the fluid had filled both lungs by the time it was heard by doctors. She was hospitalized immediately, but the doctors expected to have it under control in a week or so. Jim and I happened to be in town, having flown in for a scheduled visit with her. Along with my dad, we broke every hospital-visiting rule to stay by her side in shifts. Mom was too slow on the computer to rely on it, so we were often needed to translate her needs to the nurses. Yet she remained patient and serene.

On her second day in the hospital, my father had several long loving visits with her, as had we. Right after Jim and I put aside the Scrabble board, my brother arrived with his wife and two young children. Seeing her grandchildren caused Mom to light up, and they hugged her enthusiastically. Jim and I offered to take the kids away with us so my brother and his wife could have a quiet visit with her. Soon after we kissed her good-bye and left with the children, Mom took her last breath in my sister-in-law's arms.

Although her doctors and her family had not suspected she was so close to death, we cannot help but wonder if she had a choice in the timing. That last day Mom saw every family member who lived nearby. And was it really just good fortune that I happened to fly in for a visit that week?

I lost more than a mother—she was to me a bosom friend and a model of divine grace in human form. Yet much as I wish she were still here today, I could not wish her any more weeks or months of struggle against her deadly disease. My mother died when she could play no more, when life was no longer fun. I will remember always her final request to "play for me" as her benediction upon me. I will play Scrabble for her, sensing her delight in every new word formed. I will play on the wilderness trails she so loved, feeling the reverberation of her triumphant hiking boots behind me. I will play on dance floors, seeing her full skirts whirl as my father twirled her around.

And as I play each game—most important, the sacred game of life she reveled in so fully—I will be inspired by the courage that my mother shared with all. The silence of death has been broken by her eternal message of joy, words she never spoke aloud that echo daily in my head and heart.

DEMETER'S UNDOING

Phyllis Capello
Persephone was abducted, taken from the light.
But some daughters go willingly, renaming the darkness love, they step down.

He bought her with trinkets, an ounce or two
of affection; her heart fluttered; she did not
recognize the serpent's twist in his smile.
The night he told her disobedient girls
were buried in the mountains, she dreamed their bones
glowed in the dark earth like weak lanterns, that
their peasant fathers cried out to the Madonna
and crossed themselves as they floated by.
So when the devil bent to unlace her shoes,
she did not object and went two days barefoot.

The morning he returned, parcel of new clothes
in one hand, vanished shoes in the other,
she put aside her dreams and lay with him.
Shivering, she rose to dress;
this time he bent to lace her shoes.
They drove through the village; the mothers
hurried their daughters away; everyone knew:
he was the wicked prince in the golden coach,
she, his expendable princess.

Quick as gold spun from straw, heroin hidden
in shoes has made him rich; but when this
señorita arrives (the airport dogs run,
sniffing and yelping at her heels) she yields
to the customs search.

In the old story, domination
is a metaphor for passion.
The long, narrow windows of the county jail
shimmer at night; cell by cell,
each woman recalls her passage: the politics
of arousal, the consequence of persuasion,
the sad, seductive foreplay of submission.

ROCKETS TO EARTH

Pat Hennon

In her early twenties
she shot her eyes
straight up
into the clouds

Wild eyed kid
didn't understand
how that brick
hit her head

She fell down hard
but jumped up quick
like it really
didn't happen

Those were mistaken years
spent in bathroom stalls
tying off
her wasted arm

Pumping yellow rockets
into her veins
into the street
the rush of her life

Once she laid down
under a white ceiling
shaking her bones
to death

She knew for sure
someone was lowering
German shepherds
out the upstairs window

They did this on purpose
just to get her, you know,
for she didn't get it
gotten by her own rage

It must have been the speed,
or the good and bad acid,
or the Mad Dog wine
that held her together

On a fast rocket always
all night long
in and out of clever jazz songs
or a bright angel's gibberish

Faster and faster she went
until one rotten day
she stopped and walked real slow
back to the living room window

This time she let the German shepherds
come inside, to face her alone,
while she shook in her own stark fear
This wasn't another mistake

CROSSES AND CANDLES

Susan Cameron

Lights up on a church. The sounds of a thunderstorm wail outside. A WOMAN dashes through the door. She is soaking wet, and has a dripping newspaper on her head. She carries a gym bag over her shoulder and a manila envelope in her hand. She dumps the bag and newspaper on the floor, and pushes her wet hair out of her eyes. She sees that the envelope is wet and reacts. She picks up her things and sits hurriedly in the front pew. She opens the envelope and pulls out a contract. She glances around and pulls out a manuscript, checking to see that it is dry. She pulls a towel from her gym bag and dries the contract. She then attempts to dry her face and hair. She catches sight of the crucifix straight out front. She puts the towel down, folds her hands, closes her eyes and attempts to pray. After a moment, she gives up and speaks suddenly—

WOMAN

Listen. It's raining—my shoes are squishing—I'm here to get out of the storm, ok? And I've been trying to talk to you in my head, but I'm having enough trouble convincing myself you're actually present here... and thinking that you're listening to my thoughts. So, if I could just talk out loud, well... at least I could believe I'm listening even if you're not.

Or even if you don't exist.

I'm sorry to say—but that's a big factor here. That's kind of sad... I mean, you do exist—even if in the realm of doubt. And, if I'm wrong—there are these places and people who believe—and if they're right, then considering all you've done, you must be saying, "Ingrate!" Not that you say. Maybe I'm just not tuning into the right channel. Maybe I'm standard cable and you're Pay-Per-View, but I don't hear... Sorry for the analogy... Look, I'll go in a minute. I have a contract to Xerox. You know of a copy shop around here? My first almost-published book. *(She picks up the manuscript and reads.) Moral Bankruptcy and Western Culture*—just wanted to share that with you. Any comments? *(She starts to put the book in her bag and discovers her sneak-*

118

ers.) I have to take off these goddamn shoes. Oh. Sorry… "Sorry." You know, I apologize for everything… somehow, I think you're involved. Any comments? *(She pulls out a sock and then another one. They don't match. She searches for the match to either, then sighs and puts the unmatched ones on.)* I was once told by one of your aberrant penguins that I would burn in hell for eternity for wearing mismatched socks… As I stood in the trash can in the corner of the first grade classroom… Anyway, you just have to understand the aversion I have to rosaries, churches, bleeding statues of all kinds… Matched socks… well, basically anything representing authority—I became allergic at an early age. And I don't really know what to do here. I mean, I remember—the kneeling, the sign of the cross, the castigation and so on, but —"Whereas the party of the first part"—me—"has said Major Reservations"—how do we negotiate? Could we speculate? I don't know about you, but I've been doing that. It's become… my religion.

Do you? Speculate? On what you've done? How you've failed? Like the part where she tempts him—that was a good one. "She made me eat the apple." If you're going to line the sexes up at the starting gate and fire the gun, don't give her a ball and chain to run with. Or maybe it's just all… entertainment—"Hey, seventh day, I'm a little cranky, I've got a pair of Humans I just made, let me just stick a great big Question Mark on their foreheads." Presto! Millennia worth of re-runs to entertain! *(She picks up the manuscript.)* Chapter Three—"The Effect of Free-Thinking on the Decline of Western Culture"—needs a re-write, my editor says… *(She stuffs the manuscript and contract in her bag.)*… She's right. How can you write about something you've never done? It may be entertainment to you, but speaking from experience, it's just not that funny—the puzzle of, the analysis of… Oh, and thank you for Mortality—for the knowledge of that. Thank you for that. *(She kneels, folds her hands and says flatly,)* My mother has cancer. If you haven't heard a word of this, hear this. Let her live. *(Long pause.)* So. How was that, for you? *(She stands and starts to go. The sound of the rain stops her.)* Look—it's pouring. I'll go soon, I just… I was hoping it would be… nice here, you know? Maybe that's why we start all prayer with a cross—an "X' across the Question Mark—"In the name of a faith, we obliterate the questions… *(She sits back down.)* God? I'm attempting to switch channels here… God? Could you turn off the mute button, please? I'm talking. It's contract time… and I'm talking… I'll give up the doubts… and I'll come here every day and bow to your rules… I'll do… anything—if you can just tell me, somehow, that she'll be O.K.…

Maybe language is just— … And we scramble and fight to understand—and none of it matters. I mean, you make the rules and we have to come in here out of the rain and (Pause) And avoid reality… Any comments? I didn't think so. *(She folds the envelope and newspaper, and packs them in her bag.)* I need to go back to the office. There are reports, phone calls, faxes, lots of words I need to answer—and there isn't enough space in this mind you cursed with a Question to ask myself—anything—in the middle of all the phone calls I'm getting. So I just thought—it was raining—I thought… I don't know why. *(She sees the row of votive candles in front of her.)* Except that as I passed by the door, I saw candles... Depending on the extent of your reality, you may or may not know this... Six years old, my dog's been hit by a car on my birthday, and my mother lit the candles and sang Happy Birthday, and I wished and blew them out. I wished and my dog lived. That simple. So, I'm asking... *(She kneels, picks up a match and slowly lights the candles.)* In the name of the six year old that is buried under the questions... *(She lights a candle.)*... And of the hope, which is the only prayer I still believe in... *(She lights another.)*... And of the power... *(She lights another.)*... in the ability to love... *(She lights another.)* Amen.

(She holds the match in front of her. She closes her eyes and wishes. She blows out the match. Blackout.)

"THE PROBLEM OF CHANGE..."

Colleen M. Webster

...was the dominant theme of her literary life"
and the effort of concealment is the theme
of literature concerning her life.

Willa,
I read your pioneers and immigrant farmers
and smelled the soil and love of Nebraska
in your words. You wrote a fine line
about that prairie land, growing wheat,
stubborn oxen people, rooted, rock-like
in traditions that would never accept
your "sharing a bedroom with Edith."
What changes would have to be made
to have allowed you to name your love,
take her hand and lead her through the vast
and unbending land of your country?

You wore the proper, high-collared dress,
posed stern-faced for photographs, alone,
and never peopled your novels with
anything but child-bearing marrieds.
So you gathered your long skirts
safely across the fields of history,
but forged no new paths for those
brave, voiceless women to come.

O, what pioneers in sexuality and truth
could have been enough for this cold earth?

Five decades from your death,
in the same, unchanging Nebraska, Teena
is shot and left to die seven days after
pleading with police to investigate
her rape and beating by the men
who eventually kill her.

                                   I wonder
If she had the chance to read your
Antonia, if she had the chance to
read the warnings of a land with no
mercy, no change, and no tolerance.
Teena didn't grace your prairies with
flowing skirts and bustles—"she dressed
like a man" the papers report, and again
I wonder. What is like a man? Did she
wear khakis, Levis, button-downs, vests,
low shoes, t-shirts, the occasional tie,
belt, suspenders?

                              The papers carried
her photograph, a face I liked immediately.
A roguish, rough-and-ready smile spread
across her tawny face. There were sure,
strong cheekbones and soft dimples. She
was no man. She was beaten, raped,
ignored and eventually shot to death
one cold Christmas Day in Falls City
because, like you, Willa, she shared
a bedroom with a woman.

I, too, write words that may fail
to bring the change we need to live,
write our words, and love women, but,
I will name us. Willa, you loved Isabelle,
then Edith. Teena would have loved perhaps
a Mary or Vanessa or Sherilyn. And I love
my own Stacey. We take sweaters, boots,
Levis, and t-shirts out of closets, choosing
what to wear into our difficult future
where we will break a land and people of deep
rooted beliefs that could kill us.

O, what pioneers in sexuality and truth
will be enough for this cold earth?

In memoriam for Willa Cather (1873–1947)
and Teena Brandon (1972–1993)

THE GIFT

Sharon Charde

I am a generous woman.
I gave the world my second son.
He's not my only-begotten, I'm no virgin,
nonetheless I have offered him.
You understand, at first, there was no thought of doing this.
He walked about like any other mother's son,
swinging a backpack, wearing a tee-shirt, needing a haircut.
And I was like any other mother, choking
on the catalogue of do-it-rights, wobbling with worry.
I shared my box of scars with anyone who would listen.
I stayed with my husband.
I did not yet know how generous I would come to be,
what offering the chalice of my little life contained.
I was quite querulous at times. You know the story.
Eating the vegetables, actually pretty ordinary,
It's the next part, how I got to the giving, that you need to know.
Listen.

There is a boy striding around the Eternal City.
The phone rings.
You answer it.
There is dead silence for a long time.
The police come.
You get on a plane, fly to the other country,
learn to speak its language.
The going gets rougher.
You select a box the size of a body and decorate this box.
(I used lilacs which were blooming then.)
You listen to people saying things like, "Life goes on,"
and "God needed him," and the heels of your black pumps catch
in the soft May lawn of your home which is suddenly filled
with men and women in black dresses and good suits and food
from the neighbors. There are no children.
Someone, you, have invited these people.
It is the beginning of the generosity, a small opening.
Then the people all leave and you are left holding this, what

could I call it, outline, maybe, of a person, your child, who was
someone who lived and breathed in the house behind the lawn.
You have to go into the house.
You have to live there.
You start seeing things, think about how maybe he'll just walk out
from behind the oak tree, the one the wooden swing hangs from,
and say hello mom it's not true, none of it.
You have dreams.
Your hair turns gray in one week.
All openings close.

Then after a long time, (I really don't know how long)
you hear something that sounds like music.
You walk down a long dirt road through bayberry
with a black dog bounding towards an ocean you can hardly see
but know is up ahead.
You begin to collect stones, white ones, not black ones.
put them on your window sills. You begin
to give the stones to other people.
You learn to strip shingles off an old building
and put new ones on.
You invite people to this building so they can share
your view of the water and see the white stones.
You add feathers, shells.
Sit in the sun in summer.
You feel fortunate, and know
your cup runneth over.

When Horses Black Plumed Come

Dorrit A. O'Leary

When horses black plumed come
the long shuttered automobile at the door
let there be no eulogy
no pompous incantation

Let there be laughter and gaiety
a dry martini onion pearled
fifth of Beethoven

Sing, women who may attend
wear bright blue silken dresses
men in dungarees
plucking softly each
guitars in bluegrass melodies

At the grave release
a clutch of crows
against the sky

this will be the celebration
Mine and Ours

CHAPTER SIX

GIFTS FROM THE EARTH

What's the rush? The temple is not the goal.
It is just the journey. There's nowhere to go.

Trees, wind, water, sky,
the cave and mountains run deep in my body,
and so life will flow and just be,
by being life.

No trip, no goal, just journey,
I am being prayed by the earth,
here now,
hear now.

THE GOOD NEWS

for the mosquitoes of Minnesota
Alice Friman

I managed to make them
very happy.
Whenever I went out
lilies opened on their pads
like satellite dishes
and butterflies
spread their flags
to flutter the good news. I was
the Red Cross rolling in
in a white truck—
donuts and blankets
sacks of rice & powdered
milk for the babies. I was
payday for the troops
R & R and a geisha
for Saturday nights, Lucky Strikes
and a kiss before dying.
I was the Berlin airlift
and the Marshall Plan—
chicken soup in vats
and a hunk of bread, ripped off
with the back teeth. I was
hope for the young
and succor for the old
and after me, surely
faith in a second coming
for it is I who answered
their wing & their prayer
who gathered to me
the whining dispirited
and unified the multitudes.
It is for me the cathedrals
for me the bells
for I am the miracle

the sacrificial lamb.
I am the staff of life
the bread basket of this world
the loaves and fishes
the body and the blood.

DIARY OF AN ALCOHOLIC

Hestia Irons

4:30 a.m. The alarm goes off. I look forward to getting up. I fix Paul's lunch and make his coffee, but my reason for the happiness I feel is having my tall refreshing drink of orange juice heavily laced with Smirnoff.

I continue drinking all day, controlling it as best I can to remain functional. Today I have an appointment at a center where they help alcoholics get treatment. I don't want to go. I sit sipping yummy lemonade, almost as if savoring my last hours with a lover: my abusive lover who coaxes me with promises of peace and happiness, and does deliver—only to turn and torture me with demands of depression and anxiety. How can he have such control over me while I live here in such a perfect environment for recovery? I put him off as long as I can and then totally give in because his allure is stronger than anything else I have ever known. The warm relief flowing down my throat overtakes me, and "peace." For now. Later the demons return, whether my lover is with me or not. Nothing can protect me from the torment, the fear until I sleep—not sweet restful sleep, but sleep with bizarre dreams, tossing, grinding my teeth. Why do I keep returning to him—destruction of self, my fear of being without, my fear of being discovered?

I look in the mirror at a bloated face, bloodshot eyes, a swollen body. I take my thirty-day, one-year, two-year coins that I earned going to AA from my key ring and toss them in a drawer. To Thine Own Self Be True.

I walk in old shoes, tight clothes, a coat with a broken zipper. He is most important. He is more a necessity to me than anything else. When I walk into the liquor store, I wonder if they notice my broken shoes, my old coat, my shaky hands as I write out a check, the burns on my arms from tending the fire while drunk.

I feel sick to my stomach as I swallow my third drink, and I get mad because I want to keep drinking, keep swallowing, taking him into me, hold him close one last time. His hold is so powerful.

When I wake from my drunken sleep, I feel like a "sad, old, wrinkled balloon." My flight, my beauty, my color are all stolen from me.

No one hears my pain, my emptiness, my longing for fulfillment. Food—give me food, give me drugs, sex, fill the emptiness with sweet, sweet relief, even if it is only temporary. I hear the clock ticking, marking time, chiming the hour. I know no time at this point, only the shadows changing on the walls as the sun moves by and the flicker of light on the waves.

I play soft piano music that touches a part of me, that releases something in my tortured soul, and I cry.

I had to stop or die, so I performed a ritual, turning my life over to the Goddess.

Cloaking my naked body, I walk a path to a fallen tree that has a huge hole inside its bark. I look into that hole, the womb of Mother Earth. I put myself into the hole, into the womb, and sit silent a long time. I sit submerged in the fresh dirt, the birthing blood of Mother. I wait with mixed feelings; shedding old habits, then cry out to the Goddess to let me be born again without the pain of addiction. I rise up without my security cloak. I must do this in total nakedness, and begin my journey through the birthing root. The rough bark scratches my skin. I want to hurt and bleed and pull myself through, transformed.

After, I dress in virgin white and stand in the lake offering a bouquet of beautiful dead weeds from the fields where I walk. I offer up my death and symbolic rebirth, wrapped in my celestial cape of stars, gazing into the beauty of new life.

It's twenty-four days now that I have not had alcohol. I walk into the woods. My awareness is heightened with colors, scents, the feel of the earth beneath my bare feet. The Goddess blesses me by sending a fox trotting across my path. The dogs frighten a blue heron, which flies above my head. I hear the sound of her wings. It's as though she speaks to the center of my being. As I walk, I ask each tree, each rock, each flower for healing. Heal my soul. Allow me to open up to the Goddess and give back my strength, my power, my beauty. I chant and call, "Isis, Astarte, Diana, Hecate, Demeter, Kali, Inanna," to keep negative thoughts from my mind.

I lie on a small hill warmed by the sun, covered with soft pine needles that have fallen there year after year. They give under my weight and it feels like an embrace. I lay my arms under my head and cry into the earth. My tears and pain are absorbed. Mother Earth heals. I look up and see my dogs gathered around. I see the Goddess reflected in their eyes, and I know I have begun my journey out of darkness.

NEW WORLDS

Joanna C. Scott

We speak our souls
in riddles to each other,
converse of this
while understanding that
the lightness of our touch,
our swift averted glances,
skim like water beetles
across a slick reflective surface
below which a heavy metaphor
dissolves and rises in a fizz
of fragile minute globes,
each one carrying
a new world.

INTHENOW

Cynthia G. La Ferle

In the now, on a bike ride in July,

there is only the blur of weathered
gray pickets/yellow hollyhocks/a green door.
Heat broils the pavement; a sudden breeze kicks up some relief.
Speeding down Catalpa, chrome flashes;
wheels click into another gear.

The future curls up, blows away to pant somewhere else,
maybe under a porch with a dog named Progress.

In the now there are no
deadlines; no treatises to read or write or mail to Des Moines.
        Words roll like tumbleweed, freeflow, waiting for
    Sunday poets to catch them, then let them go.
There is breathing space, in the now, between the heat wave and
    the infinite pulse of a moment.
        There is no chore undone, not one apple to scrub.
Only old bones to discard.

Later is an odd word, the shadow of perhaps. And just now
    a phone rings on the next block for someone else to answer.

Just now, in the painted wooden bungalows waft symphonies
        composed of one hundred and three new aromas:
            Vegetable stew and Mozart,
                a thousand velvet bees
        and dark purple petunias
            in the summer kitchen.

Look at the life spilling like pirate's treasure from terracotta pots as
though, maybe,
just maybe
    blooming for its own sake is all that matters.

In the now there are angels, some without wings.
    They leap through screen doors and crawl through
        open windows.
With tiny feet firmly rooted in the sand on the playground
    they whisper secret messages from a spirit world that hums
        Only in the now.

SAFE HOUSE

Joan McMillan

Rain begins around a woman
who puts both hands in the earth of her garden.
Into its clay and dust, she has worked compost,
humus, bag after bag of peat moss.
Now there are lavender cosmos with blank yellow eyes,
the wax-red bowls of a Chinese bellflower,
and Iceland poppies, some still in bud,
some unfolding their petals,
pink tissue paper on black-lashed stems.

She knows the value of these days,
light rising golden as bread in an aura of heat
or dulling to afternoons like this one,
the clouds a smudged charcoal landscape.

A year ago, the man she called *husband*
chased her across the driveway,
curses hemorrhaging from their mouths,
his fist slamming into her nose, her jaw,
the pillow of her belly, a long road of bruises

that ended in her kitchen as she stepped yet again
into the unseen chasm of his rage,
dishes flying from his hands and shattering,
a splintering hailstorm of glass.
That night in a women's shelter,
she covered her children with white comforters,
her life a blankness also, one she did not know how to fill

except to kneel every day, planting seedlings from flats,
small roots holding tight to the soil,
a labor of water and darkness,
until slowly, a prism of new leaves, new flowers,
and the soft silver threads of the rain on her skin.

BLUE-FOOTED MEMORIES

Ruth Innes

he pair of blue-footed boobies performed their courtship dance. Both male and female displayed their bright blue feet, holding up first one and then other for their mate's approval. Then they pointed their beaks and tails at the sky and whistled ("skypointing," our guide told us).

We were in the middle of their nesting grounds and boobies were all around us. Our presence didn't disturb them in the least as we walked through the colony. "Stay strictly on the trail," our guide in the Galapagos Islands warned. "We want to keep the birds that nest here happy and if you step off the trail even a little it may destroy a nesting site." To those of us used to northern birds like the robin, the nests weren't proper nests at all, but just a clear spot on the ground or a depression in a stone. A few nests were practically on the trail. In fact, one baby booby reached out and pecked at my foot as I went by.

I heard what the guide said, and my eyes were on the boobies, but I couldn't really appreciate their strange, delightful dance. What I kept seeing in my mind's eye, was the pitiful scene that greeted us on the beach when our dinghy first landed. A large sea lion had just given birth to a pup. We saw her nuzzling the pup, trying to make it move, but the pup was dead. Already a couple of Galapagos hawks perched nearby on the rocks. They knew they'd have a meal soon.

"It's just nature," our guide told us as he led us away from the beach to the birds' nesting grounds. "Not all the babies can live or the beach would be too crowded."

As we walked away, I couldn't stop looking back over my shoulder. The mother sea lion prodded insistently at the pup. She seemed determined to make it live again.

"Stop, give up," I wanted to call to her. But in the back of my mind was the hope that maybe, just maybe, if she pushed and prodded hard enough, she could rekindle the spark of life.

The guide tried to hurry us along the rough lava boulders and we balanced first on one foot and then the other. We saw marine iguanas so well camouflaged we could hardly distinguish them on the rocks, the masked boobies, and even an amorous pair of albatross doing their mating dance. It was wonderful and I thoroughly enjoyed seeing them. But when we came upon the blue-footed boobies showing each other their feet I felt an old familiar lump settle in my chest and I had trouble breathing.

It wasn't just the mother sea lion with her dead baby I kept seeing. I saw my son, Bobby, so long ago, with blue swim fins on his feet, as he danced around the living room, chanting, "I'm a blue-footed boobie, I'm a blue-footed boobie." His giggle was infectious and I laughed as I caught him to give him a kiss. He soon wriggled free to continue his wild fling, pretending to be the blue-footed bird whose mating habits we had watched together on a National Geographic special.

Bobby could never again pretend to be a blue-footed booby, or come with me to see a blue-footed booby. A sudden, virulent infection killed him when he was only three years old. He died in my arms in the hospital, saying nothing but "mommy" and I couldn't make him understand I was right there with him. When he stopped breathing I kept kissing him as though I could kiss life back into his body.

"There was nothing more anyone could do," the doctor told me. "It's no one's fault. We did all we could."

But I blamed myself. I should have realized how sick he was. I should have gotten him to the hospital earlier. I should have done something different! The doctor kept assuring me that no one could have done anything, but I didn't believe him.

My husband blamed me, too, or I felt he did, and we began attacking each other. Within a year we were divorced. Life continued, years went by and I tried to forget by shutting that bitter loss away in a cold, closed room of my life. Then, on that island, thousands of miles from home, I felt that familiar sharp-edged lump in my chest again as the blue-footed boobies held up their feet.

My trip to the Galapagos Islands was supposed to be a treat to myself for getting through the last few years. I wanted to see those enchanted islands, where time stood still ever since I first heard about Darwin formulating his theory of evolution there. But seeing one of the things I'd looked forward to most, the blue-footed boobies doing their courtship dance, brought back that special memory of Bobby and the hurt overwhelmed me.

I walked behind the rest of the group as we moved slowly through the nesting grounds, hoping nobody would notice how close I was to breaking down. The salty, unshed tears in my eyes made the going treacherous over the uneven terrain and I stumbled several times. The guide, concerned, came back to make sure I was all right and I pretended I was fine, just a little tired.

By the time we got back to the sea I had myself under control again. When we stopped to watch the marine iguanas ejecting salt water through their nostrils, I foolishly thought perhaps that was their way of crying for some past loss.

On the beach where the dinghy was to pick us up, we were in time to see the mother sea lion finally give up trying to coax her pup to life. She turned her back and immediately the two waiting Galapagos hawks landed next to the pup and began feasting.

Several members of our group started to chase the hawks away but the guide stopped them. "It's nature's way," he said, and we watched sadly as the hawks tore at the pup's body. The mother sea lion looked back at her pup, gave one soft bark and waddled away down the beach. She had done all she could.

Maybe I had, too.

SALTY WOMEN

Lyn Bleiler

A woman worth her salt...

is patient, like a bulb underground, trusting that growth is often seasonal.

embraces loved ones gently, the way a vine of night-blooming jasmine tiptoes around a tree.

collects lines proudly on her face, like a redwood spinning rings.

stores perfume outside her door in stalks of lavender crystal.

wears earth-colored nail polish caked underneath.

thinks of makeup as war paint and would prefer to skip the battle.

cares more for combing beaches than combing her hair.

feels that clothes, like good wine, are better when seasoned.

thinks that a heart when worn on one's sleeve makes a most attractive accessory.

has been in enough close shaves to prefer stubble.

understands that weeds have a life of their own and respects them for it.

knows that you can't make angels in snow that's been shoveled.

invites spiders to live in her corners, lets them hang lace and calls them by name.

heeds the warning that if one makes one's bed one must lie in it.

realizes that cleansers are abrasive.

ponders the polka-dot patterns rain paints on her windows.

takes comfort in the knowledge that dust settles.

believes that fur balls, left undisturbed, become kittens.

knows that brooms are vehicles for witches.

FULL OF SWEET ROSES

Vivina Ciolli

Breasts you hardly matter.

Springtime breasts, hiccups on my chest
not filling double A cups
held by elastic strap across my back
to snap, unsnap—a talisman,
bothersome rag.

Ah, cleavage. Ah, silhouette.
Sweater set pearl-buttoned down back,
head held high, shoulders erect.
Summer breasts, you are squatters
having moved in insisting on permanence.
Breasts, voluptuous, private,
eavesdropping on each inhale, eavesdropping
on my heart.

Chocolate nipples, sweet treats
for lips, for hands, for viewing
in full-length mirrors,
I sing to you uneven breasts
heavy, fall fruit. The left
below the right, planted off line
with an eye for beauty.

Winter breasts you are sourdough old crones
with whiskers, set in your ways.
I am my breasts, these children
who never leave home.

If the family seed ripens,
if sprouts take root
in these winter bearers, breasts
I will give you up to a surgeon's knife,
harvest your seasons' bounties
back to spring's flat landscape

embroidered with scars: bouquets of red roses.

MEETING THE EAGLE

Susan D. Anderson

I dressed in a hurry, trying to beat the sunrise. If I made it out to the deck in time, I could shoot a scene for my record of Flying Point Island, this scatter rug of rock dwarfed by the surrounding rotunda of Casco Bay.

Bulked up with padding from my sweatsuit, ski socks and heaviest coat, I tilted over the sink to check the thermometer outside the kitchen window. Twelve below zero; typical for the coast of Maine in January. Which camera to use? I grabbed the one Uncle Ralph loaned me, a reliable Sears model with a nearly finished roll of film. "No time for the tripod," I decided.

That first intake of brittle air made the hair inside my nostrils stiffen in alarm. My boots detonated on the trampled snow, each crystal-crushing step an intrusion in the dawn stillness. The sun was a minute or less from backlighting two small islands across the bay: Sow and Pigs to the left, Bustin's to the right. Between me and those islands lay the winter beac—a mass of white frigidity.

My ungloved hand, wooden in the sub-zero air, fumbled at the camera. As the sun cleared the horizon, the tall pine trees would chop the light into julienne strips, giving the seascape a moment of character and color. I knew that now—the way I knew how long a cord of wood lasted, and which cries in the night meant an owl had found its prey, and when to look for wisps of sea smoke. I had been sitting in front of the picture window every day for a year and a half, writing and observing.

Last year I had no camera. It didn't matter; the sights worth documenting always caught me by surprise. I was an environmental greenhorn here, unprepared for any response beyond standing stock still and letting the novelties of wilderness life rock me to the core. Taught by time and experience, I returned with a tripod, light meter and *two* cameras, one with a telephoto lens for capturing the waterfowl and seals that bobbed far from shore.

To my friends back on dry land I'd confided, "Of all the wildlife I've seen, of all the environmental drama I've witnessed, the picture I covet most is of an eagle." The first time I saw one, I was heading out with a bucket of ashes from the woodstove. I turned and gasped as I caught sight of that unmistakable white head and shoulders right there, resting on the snowy branch of a tree at the edge of the woods, no more than twenty feet away. I held my breath and remained stooped over the ash bucket as if paralyzed while I watched the eagle take off toward Bustin's with a languorous thrust of its wings.

Another day I looked up from my writing to see an eagle fly parallel to the shoreline and low over the jagged mini-bergs, even with my line of sight, again not twenty feet from where I sat. A conquered seagull, beak open as if to scream, one broad gray wing gripped by each yellow talon, dangled below it—spreadeagle, so to speak—like airborne baggage.

"Just once," I said to myself all year, "Just once I'd like to be out there with the camera all loaded and ready to go when an eagle happens by."

This particular morning, however, the eagle far back in my consciousness, I focused single-mindedly on the scene I came out to shoot. Between the distant tree trunks the sun poked rosy strips of horizontal softness, laying them gently across the stark white bay: an act of tenderness. I clicked off two shots of the scene I'd envisioned, saving film for another day and gloating a little over how easy it had become to anticipate the right timing and environmental conditions for the photographs I wanted. Then I spotted the eagle.

It flew diagonally toward me, its shape in flight and the slow rhythm of wing beats familiar to me now. And I was out on the deck with the camera loaded and ready to go. Except I had the wrong camera. I needed the one with the telephoto lens because the eagle was flying fairly high. I raced back into the house, dumped Uncle Ralph's camera with my left hand and grabbed the other camera with my right.

What a relief to see the lens already attached. Excited to the point of shaking, I sped outside, not bothering to close both doors against the cold. The eagle was midway between me and Bustin's and I aimed the camera for my first glorious shot.

Except that going into the heated house and out again fogged my glasses. I couldn't see a thing. Frantic to get the photograph—what if this was my only chance?—I swiped my glasses with my woolen scarf and whipped the camera into position, ready to follow the eagle through the lens until I framed a great picture. Except the eagle's flight path put it against the woodsy backdrop where it didn't show up as it would against blue sky or the snow-covered ice pack. And it had flown too far for the lens to fill a photograph with it. At best it would show up as a brown speck that only I could identify with a magnifying glass. I went inside and started to laugh.

I said I wanted to be there with my camera loaded and ready to go, but I forgot to say which camera. I forgot to say, "Please don't let my glasses fog," and "Please put the eagle against sea or sky for contrast," and "Please have it fly close enough for the camera to do it justice." While I was in the midst of learning about a universe filled with surprises, I carried an old assumption that I could manage and control my environment to achieve the things I wanted. The universe gave me everything I asked for, and sent the eagle to teach me that *I am not in charge.* I am not in charge of when eagles fly and where. I'm responsible for cultivating my powers of observation and for staying alert, but I cannot call forth the sights I want to see.

By mid-morning, thick clouds rolled in from the west and the wind blew mightily against the house, spoiling my plan to chop kindling. I shrugged. "I'm not in charge of the weather."

I walked across the causeway to dig out the car and pick up the mail, finding a letter of rejection from a publisher. "I am not in charge of what priorities publishers have at the moment they receive my query. I am only in charge of learning my craft and approaching publishers in a professional manner." Peace came over me as I shoveled away the latest snow drift whipped around my car by coastal winds obedient to the command of some power other than my own.

I took my new attitude on a twenty-mile drive to the grocery store on the mainland, where the brussel sprouts I wanted for dinner, but wasn't in charge of ordering, weren't available. Driving home behind a slow-moving sedan with an elderly man at the wheel, I put the brakes on my customary impatience and pictured that gentleman and me living out our ordinary days nestled inside the palm of the same cosmic hand.

For the first time in my life, I was letting go of a thousand details of daily living. A sense of joint custody, a willing partnership with the universe replaced my pretense of being the sole custodian of myself, of the space I inhabited, of events unfolding within that space. And I surrendered to the universe the details that rightfully belonged to it.

REFLECTIONS FROM A HOLY PLACE

Mary Diane Hausman

Mary left her mark because she
Dared to
Open herself to the Divine

And if we come from that Holy Sacred Center
Ma, Mother, Maya,
We are already Divine

The only redemption
We need is to become the Void
Of our own pain

To feel the pull once again of
That sacred cord that holds us
In a great womb of flowing power
In the arms of Kali-Ma

Without meeting
The Destroyer
We cannot meet
The Life-Bringer

We flow out from Darkness
On sacred red waters;

We are borne on Lotus petals and lilies;
We rise,
Dakinis
Skywalkers.

We walk the face of Ma
And looking in Her
Shining waters,
We see the face
Looking back

Is our own.

I Don't Have Faith, But…

Beverly Tricco

The Earth
In every muscle and bone that helps me stand erect
Has been here forever.
I am the dust of the stars.
My flesh has been…

    the paddies tended by thin yellow peasants
    the groves sanctified by ancient magic
    the stones that fly from a young boy's hand into bottomless pools
    countless pumpkins carved by frazzled parents
    bubbling black lava that brings new fertility
    a manicured lawn where well-groomed ladies sip tea
    and all the bodies that return to the earth to rejoin the cycle.
They are the matter of my life.
    How can I help but feel holy?

The Air
In every breath I pull into my body
Has been here forever.
I am the dust of the stars.
My air has been…

    the breeze lifting the veils of a queen waiting at a tower
    window
    the sighs of young men in love
    the morning chants of cloistered clerics
    the shouts of Scot warriors running naked into battle
    the wind that filled the sails in the age of discovery
    the whispers of furtive lovemaking
    the cries of hungry babes that refuse to be ignored.
They are the stirring of my life.
    How can I help but feel holy?

The Fire

In every pulse and beat of my tireless heart

Has been here forever.

I am the dust of stars.

My fire has been...

    the fury of a bear sow with cubs

    the stabbing of paint onto an empty canvas

    the passion of the martyrs being dragged to a stake

    lightning splitting a murderous sky

    the fist raised in triumph

    the explosive rage of the long downtrodden

    the obsession of the inventor ignoring another sunrise

    the primal mating urge.

They are the thrust of my life.

    How can I help but feel holy?

The Water

In every pulsating cell of my body

Has been here forever.

I am the dust of the stars.

My water has been...

    the well where gossiping matrons fill their buckets

    the sheets of rain where children run shrieking

    the sweat on a farmer's brow

    the fetid river baptizing brown pilgrims

    the urine of wolf cubs licked away by their mother

    the wetness of kisses

    the fluids that have cradled every baby born to earth.

They are ebb and flow of my life.

    How can I help but feel holy?

    How can I help but feel holy?

CHAPTER SEVEN

GIFTS OF THE CHILDREN

I wore a medicine pouch my mother gave me
and a crystal necklace that was my grandmother's,
and the Guatemalan jacket given to me by my dad.
They are medicine: clothes, colors and jewelry
passed down from the ones who have come before,
passed on to the children who follow.

Walking the earth with the children in mind,
we are all midpoints,
the center-full present
between what was
and what will be.

There is power and joy in this center.

WITH NO APOLOGY TO ST. PAUL

Nita Penfold

When I was a child
I spoke as a child
I danced as a child
but now that I am a woman
I hold the things of that child dear.
I cherish them and remember them,
for whosoever cannot touch the things
of the child within,
cannot enter Heaven.
And I say to you,
keep close the child
for she knows the way to God.

When Your Body Betrays You

Helene LeBlanc

One late afternoon my bedroom door opened slowly and a three-foot apparition in patent leather shoes stood in the doorway. She advanced hesitantly to the bed. I saw pale strands of hair framing a worried face. She took a deep breath and delivered the message.

"I'm suppose to find out if you want coffee or tea with your dinner so we can fix the tray." Her voice was solemn with her rehearsed words.

I knew why they had sent my youngest to my bedroom. The rest of my family felt uncomfortable around me. Since coming home from the hospital, my husband and children avoided looking directly at me when they spoke. I couldn't blame them.

I beckoned Susie closer and patted the side of the bed. She seemed to be struggling for something to say. Her little fingers made swirling designs on the blanket but stopped when she came near my arm. Had she been told not to touch me?

"Susie," I murmured, "Is something bothering you? You know you can ask me anything."

She looked straight at me, frowning slightly, the way she did when she wanted a straight answer. She asked abruptly.

"Mummy? Are you going to die?"

As I stared at my child, whatever pain I felt in my body was nothing compared to the anguish I saw in her eyes.

As I held her close, I understood my family's feelings. The child had brought out the fear that hung in the house like black crepe. I needed support and love, but my own fears had closed the door between us. Now Susie, with a child's innocence, opened the door, demanding answers.

I didn't have any answers. My mind didn't want to know survival statistics. Suppose the cancer returned. Suppose the treatments didn't work. If I tell her I will be fine, she will believe me. If things don't work out, how will she react? She will feel I lied to her. Suppose, suppose, suppose. Please God, I prayed, help me. I don't have any answers and I'm scared, too.

"Honey. I don't think so. But everyone dies sometime. Everyone. Everything. The doctors said things look good. Is that what's bothering you?"

"Well. But…," She tilted her head to one side and frowned. She took another deep breath and asked. "If you die… will you wait for me there?"

The only movement in the room was my fingers tracing the small features on the upturned face. The lump in my throat kept me from speaking and I blinked to stop the hot tears. If I cried, she would be so frightened. She was asking for such a little thing. I tightened my grip and brushed her taffy-colored hair with my lips as I whispered my promise. "Yes. Yes, my darling. I will wait for you always."

Susie squirmed and I heard a muffled giggle. "I can't breathe. You're squeezing me. You're strong." She unwrapped herself from my arms and stood up. A smile danced in her eyes and she stuck out her hand. "Shake?"

I reached out and took her hand. Susie's acceptance of life and death was so simple it made me smile. It had been my own fear that created the shadows of feeling alone and abandoned. That fear, combined with a "Why me!" anger, had closed out the love and support I needed. A rush of guilt made me realize I had not asked anyone for help, even God. I realized now that I had a lot to fight for. My child was showing me the way.

She stood watching me, her bright smile making the shadows grow faint.

"I'll need your help," I said. "I have to lean on someone." I squeezed her hand again. My grip was stronger. The covenant was made.

After she left, I sat on the side of the bed and wrapped my arms around myself. I squeezed as much as possible. I dropped my chin and cried. It wasn't anyone's fault and surely not my body. I could feel my mind beginning to connect the wires, gently sending me the message that it was all right to be scared.

I don't remember how long I sat there, but it had to be whatever time my body and mind needed to work together again. What happens to women who don't have a Susie or anyone to bring them back? I thought. Outside in the hallway, I heard the sounds of living. It was time to join the world. I had a lot to do.

TO MY MOTHER

Elizabeth Cunningham

Your shoulders slump
to form a shield; you yield,
your only defense against
yielding a self you will not
name. Giving way
has become your way; your will,
denied, has gone underground:
a vein of iron.
Your anger is cold;
you call it depression.

But I am your daughter and swear
I sprang from a molten womb.
Your conformity is too complete:
I scent contempt.
I know you, war-torn woman.
With your right hand you bind me,
with your left you set me free.
I am your rebellion
embodied.
I am your silence
broken into song.

Defeat is your disguise:
within a warrior sleeps.

I am the dream.

BATHERS

Mariko Nagai

Kneeling naked, my mother asks
me to wash her back, her forearms

wearing the heat of the room. Stripping
myself, I refill the bucket, shocks

of cold encountering the humid
air; my mother settles down on the tiled floor,

a crane warning the approacher with her open
wings, her neck proud with beauty, and waits.

I circle sponge along the line of her back as round
as grief, moving down, spiral like a gull

circling down to the next. I let palmful
of water rinse her back near her purple

birthmark dulled from years of hiding.
Her head bowed down, shy—

the usual, she says, the *usual*, as she offers
her breasts. I massage two white desires

fruiting from her bowed body. One breast,
then another, I search for the lumps that may flower

out, caving the body, blossoming
her nearer to death.

Her pubic hair glistens in the folds,
tucking in neatly as the intricate weaving of crane.

And I towel her, pressing the cloth
weighing my love, droplets thieving

down between the shadowed crack
of her buttocks, and I enclose her in a towel.

BAT MITZVAH MOTHER

Wendy Goulston

My back is warmed by the breath of many I love, friends and relatives, all here to honor our daughter and bring love to our celebration of her bat mitzvah. My husband Alan gleams with excitement. Nine-year old Josh bounces, yet manages to stay more or less in his seat. Aviva, our daughter, is being initiated into her adulthood as a Jewish woman in the ways of our ancestors.

She sits tall and elegant behind the bima, gold-slippered feet tucked together. A black velvet skirt hangs gracefully over her knees. A floral silk vest highlights the black shine of her hair and eyelashes. I see a girl growing into early womanhood. My heart swells as her fingers and eyes seek the ring on her right hand.

Can Aviva tell that the pearls in her ring connect her with the women who cannot be there with her on the bima, her mother, her grandmothers, her great-grandmothers? I imagine that in fingering the ring she opens a key to an invisible realm where wise women ancestors wait to greet the initiate whose time has come to learn ancient female knowledge.

She is the first female in my family and Alan's to cantilate the full torah and haftorah portion, performing the same role as a bar mitzvah boy. She has stood for over an hour singing, circled by the men called up to punctuate her reading with blessings. Her father, cousins, uncles, parents' male friends and the fathers of her friends spiral her into the fold.

The spirit-men of my family line are split in two as they crowd around me, whispering. Eyes gleam, some with fury, some with glee. Beards nod. "Yes, yes. It is good. It is wonderful. She knows how to pray, to think, to learn. She will grow and live as a Jew." Others shake fiercely, "This is not a woman's place. The bima is desecrated."

Old spirit-women sit alertly around me, straining to hear each note. Tears flow from their eyes; mothers seek the arms and hands of daughters, sisters of sisters. Some seem angry, others awash with sadness and joy. Their quiet tears form a pool around me, a mikva whose clear purity I step into and emerge the mother of a bat mitzvah girl.

I remember discussing the role of women in our Conservative synagogue with three other bat mitzvah mothers in the rabbi's office a year ago. We long for a forbidden aliya during our daughter's bat mitzvah service. We want the important women in our daughters' lives to be called to the bima, to be a part of that ring around the Torah. But the rabbi says the congregation is not ready for women's full participation, and he points out what significant changes have already been made. We tell him our feelings about being excluded.

I feel the challenge to the old ways in my bones—the pain both of those who cling to the ancient and sanctioned laws they love, and of those who cry to be admitted into the sacred circle, knowing their spiritual wings are broken by invisible barriers pressing them to the outer borders of community rituals.

I remember discussing with Aviva how women's participation is limited. In no uncertain terms she is happy with the present state of affairs. It does not bother her one bit that girls can read Torah in the main sanctuary only on their bat mitzvah and never again. After all, she can read Torah at school services, and at other services in our synagogue, which do not take place in the main sanctuary. She likes having her Dad and male relatives on the bima with her. She wants to do just what the other girls and boys do. She certainly does not want anything embarrassingly different proposed by her mother.

It is I who feel scorched by the ancestral female silence, the absence of women's written accounts of their experience in Torah times; the void of female midrash interpreting the Torah, the historical lack of women's bodies moving and singing as they touch the Torah or lead services. No woman of my past has ever entered the man's world of the bima or of Jewish "lerning" and debate, or even of Jewish song and dance.

For months I toy with the idea of having my voice heard at Aviva's ceremony, if not in an aliya, then in a short address. Looking for support, I seek the reactions of other mothers at our synagogue. What do they think of mothers speaking from the bima to their bat mitzvah daughters? They do not want to do it. One mother silences me altogether, exclaiming, "I would not want to rob my daughter of her limelight." I decide it is best, easiest, to lay down my wish that at my daughter's bat mitzvah an older, female mother-voice might give her the blessing of a gift of words.

One day while watching the sun play with the sapphires in my ring, I realize with a jolt that the ring feeding my eyes and soul came to me in a private ritual, passed on to me from my mother, who had received it from her mother. Then I remembered my grandmother's pearl ring my mother gave me when I was thirteen. I decide to hide that ring under Aviva's pillow for her to find on the morning of her bat mitzvah, with a note expressing my feelings and wishes for her. That will have to suffice.

However as the bat mitzvah approaches, I burn anew with the pain of having to sit silent. Aviva will sing of Miriam's leading the women in music and dance, affirming God's parting of the waters for the Israelites. But there will be no Miriam leading the way to the sacred living waters for her or me; no women singing up there with Aviva, no timbrals either. This service will not give my daughter even a sip from the woman-held cup of Miriam's well.

I make a special appointment with a young rabbi whom I admire and trust. She urges me to speak in the synagogue for Aviva's sake as well as my own. But I worry about taking attention away from Aviva and embarrassing her. "I'll cry when I speak despite the effort to "pull myself together." My father and rabbi grandfather would never break down. This rabbi supports me. "Your daughter needs to know it is appropriate to be moved at such times. Tears are good to share. Besides, Aviva and the congregation need to know what you have to say. So do you." Alan, Aviva and our synagogue rabbi agree to my speaking for seven minutes about the Torah portion Aviva reads.

Great wings beat their way up my throat as my voice sweeps through the sanctuary:

"When moved with God's blessing there is enormous power in human hands and voices. Moses' hands part the seas so there is ground to walk on. His hands cast a tree into the waters so it is sweet to drink. His hands hold a rod and smite the rock that, against all possibility, yields drinking water. Just as miraculously, Miriam and the women's hands take timbrels and make music, song and dance, joyous expressive arts as crucial as ground water and weapons. The people's hands gather manna that comes with a new day when they were hungry. Their hands choose just enough for the needs of the individual, no more, no less, and they learn what is God-given so they will survive and flourish. Finally, Moshe raises his hands over the battleground so that the community can sustain its fight to live. His hands, like ours, got tired and yet stayed raised with the support of comrades.

Aviva, all his life your grandpa has used his hands and voice to make poetry and heal people, to grow flowers, vegetables and fruits. Your granny plunges her hands into the soil too. She nurtured children, prepared food, worked clay into pots and raw wool into sweaters. Your zeide has used his hands to cut meat with precision, and his voice patiently explains to hundreds of people how to use tools and choose them wisely. Your babbe uses her hands and voice to sing and tell stories, to sell clothes that bring people pleasure, to collect tzedaka money. Your mother wraps her large hands around her loved ones and lustily sings off-key. Your dad, one of the world's best huggers, uses his voice too, to gloriously sing off-key, to joke and tell his truth.

Carrying the power of your relatives and ancestors, your own strong voice and hands have always expressed themselves in your own unique way. May you continue to use them vigorously and proudly as you enter into the sweet drinking places and desert times of your adulthood."

Her bat mitzvah ushered me into my own desert where I found invisible springs feeding the riverbeds of Jewish women's souls. Women in my family did not learn Hebrew. We were not ritually welcomed into Judaism as Aviva has been. My mother is a spiritual, selectively observant woman, for all her rabbi's-daughter childhood. Her mother grew up in a non-observant home, then dedicated her life to serving her rabbi husband and community, at home and at synagogue, behind the mehitzah which divides men and women during services.

Aviva and I wear these women's rings as we address the congregation, and as we turn to be enveloped in the swirl of people whose hands and voices rush to greet us, I see our wet-eyed ancestors twinkling in the dust motes.

CITY DWELLER

Laraine Herring

he forest of pines and oaks and elms that surrounds my grandmother's white clapboard house used to be miles deep. My grand- mother remembers when alligators lived in the creek and when she added on the sun-porch after Hurricane Hazel toppled one of the bigger trees onto her roof.

It happens, I guess. The ocean crashes over million dollar summer homes and crumbles them like Mississippi slave shacks. Tornadoes blow through the same Kansas town year after year; the same trailer parks. Folks rebuild. Women clean up and repaint and start new gardens, in the same place.

I marvel at this. Why not move somewhere "safe" like Arizona or maybe Utah? "This is home," I hear them say. "This is the earth. These things happen." Maybe these women know what I have yet to learn. Nowhere is safe. We must surrender to the wind, the rain, the sun, because we can't beat them.

I am a city dweller. I make my home in a concrete square that looks just like all the other concrete squares on my block. I drive on concrete to a larger concrete structure where I work, to make money so I can go to the store and pick out my apples and oranges and pears from bins. I have a small rectangle section of grass in my backyard and I get annoyed if it dares to grow enough to warrant mowing.

I never knew tomatoes had a taste until my grandmother made tomato sandwiches for us one summer. They were fire red and thick and juicy like beef (aren't all tomatoes pale orange—even green?) With just a dab of salt they had more flavor than any salad in my organized alphabetized metropolis.

"They come from the garden," says my grandmother. Yes. So does the corn, and okra, and cucumbers, and watermelon. She knew these vegetables when they were seeds. I didn't know the difference between bushes and weeds in my new backyard. I had to buy a book to know which leafy things growing by the driveway were good, and which ones I was supposed to poison. To me, weeds look a lot like grass and clover looks a lot like it belongs.

The city is pretty at night, I tell myself, listening to cars speeding by at seventy-five miles per hour: sirens, accidents, gunshots. Death has a sound in the city. We don't even think that for every ambulance siren a life hangs in the balance. At my grandmother's house, when a siren passes by, the crystal plates are loaded with chicken and vegetables and driven down to the affected family. At home the siren is an inconvenience—a sound that wakes me up before the alarm, evoking no emotion but anger. To my grandmother, the siren is a signal for a change, a new cycle of someone's life.

I am afraid of death. I am afraid of change. In the city, we effectively halt change. We can make flowers grow year round. We exist in climate-controlled prisons occasionally stepping onto our balconies for a breath of fresh air and smelling something we can't identify, but we know. Spring? Life? It's nice, we say. It's a nice day.

In winter, my grandmother has no tomatoes. It's the wrong season, she says. I have the same shadows of fruits and vegetables I have all year. They're a few cents more in the winter, that's all. When she dies, there will be no one left in the family who can grow okra, who can preserve figs and apples. I used to pity her. Living in a house with no heat or air conditioning. We convinced her to get indoor plumbing just five years ago. Come on, Grandma, really. You don't have to suffer like this anymore. She relented, but I think it was more to shut us up than because she wanted an indoor shower.

Thank God we don't have to live like that, I thought when I was a child. Thank God I wasn't born one hundred years ago. I have learned my life will end one day. No matter how I live I will die. Most of us will die without tending our own gardens, without harvesting our own vegetables, without knowing that life is a circle, and we will be reborn like our ancestors of the earth.

My grandmother dies several weeks after my last visit. Her friends (those few who are still alive) know instinctively that she is OK. I do not share their confidence. I do not understand the cycles, the ebb and flow of life that is at my center and I look to books and tapes for answers. In spring the soil thaws and the first splashes of green poke through the earth. I didn't plant them. They just appeared. They knew to return. Perennials?

I am staying in my grandmother's house until we are able to find a buyer. I find green stamps and war bonds in the attic; old milk bottles and *Reader's Digests* in the garage. Dust belongs here. I don't clean it up. I let it be. I let many things be. I get up with the sun and go to bed shortly after dark. I am forgetting that Letterman is on at 11:30, and that the news is on at 5, 6, and 11 for my convenience. I feed a stray black cat but she doesn't love me. She is just hungry. I want to think she's my friend, but I know better. I know she's her own spirit. I let her be.

One morning I go to the nursery. I'm not sure what to ask for and I wander blindly through the rows and rows of plants until an employee takes pity on me.

"What can I help you with?" she asks and smiles. Her red lipstick doesn't fill the creases of her lips. Her eye-shadow is too blue.

"Seeds?" I say. "I need seeds."

"For what?" She's very patient.

"Life?" I say, bewildered.

"I know just what you need," she says, and we walk to the back of the store where she hands me packets of seeds—green peppers, squash, tomatoes, butter beans. "Be patient, dear. They'll grow."

"Yes," I say and smile. "I know."

FINDING FEATHERS

Laura Rogerson Moore

I was skinned knees, tree climber,
Palms laced with dirt and salt and sweat.
Lover, too, of low dark places:
Under porches, inside tall hedges—
A spider's web breaker.
I peed in the bushes, faced the wind,
Rode standing up on the pedals of my bike—
Banister slider.

I am scuffed heels, housekeeper,
Baby maker,
Filling mouths, washing bodies,
Bearing them in and out of dreams.
I am the wife of a man.
I lie beside him, hear his breath, wear his smell.
Wait like a good, patient dog,
Like a cat, a baby bird.
Something wants to run, to pounce, to be fed,
To take wing.

I will be a large, ancient woman,
Carved by age, thick with years.
I will live in the woods and
Walk naked in my yard.
The sun will warm my used breasts.
I will sing. I will whistle. I will wail.
I will wear big boots and
In the spring wade the swollen
Creeks back into the hills
To their source.

I will find feathers and put them in jars.
And when I die,
I can give them to my children.
They, too, shall fly again.

CHILDREN'S CHILDREN

Elizabeth Welles

Children hear a vision
                          Sounds of the orange sun.
           Children see a rhythm
                        Beat of an ancient drum.
      Children in creation
                        stir in Mother's womb,
        Children of our children
                        Earth is where you bloom.

From a tight little ball
           you uncurl and fall into the lap of Creation
                time and time again,
                    hurled onto a spiraled path
                            one that never ends.

Like the deer in meadow,
        wind through trees,
             you find yourself out of the Garden,
                for covering,
                    there are no leaves.
Naked, you bleed yourselves out of the womb,
        onto the Earth,
             which will one day be your tomb.

There's a heartbeat on the Earth
             the children can hear.
      It calls to the walls
             and barriers of fear.
      Wailing, beating its arms against its chest,
             this beating goes on
                      North, East, South and West.

In all the worlds
             we hear the cry,
        in all the worlds
             salvation does not die.

Children hear the songs of Earth,
     witnessing parents' passionate birth.

At first the quiet tumbling walls,
     then crashing loud,
          thunderous applause.
The beat of rain
          drops against ceiling roofs,
     and slow leaks appear,
               watering old roots.

Tears of our ancestors
          moisten brittle spaces,
     drowning out traces
          of forgotten fears,
               that made living hard and dry.
     Slowly then, we are ready to begin,
          and Earth
               She softly sighs.

Nurturing creation,
     with no push, pull or strain,
a rising foundation,
          Compassion its name,
     births a spirit remembering Mothers and Fathers,
          who are now free, spiraling home
               in Eternity.

And forgiveness
          sprouting like the sun,
spreads across lands
          where the beat of the Earth is One.

Drumming
     Drumming
               Reverberating cells,

Drumming
     Drumming
               Holy Bells.

A F T E R W O R D

S I N G   T H E   E A R T H ' S   J O Y

e sing the Earth's joy and celebrate our inseparable and symbiotic relations with the body of the earth by recognizing our life intertwined with the oceans, the trees, the mountains and air, with each species, and each other. Tasting on our lips the salt ocean air, we stand to see birds nesting; we feel their flight as wind drifts across our skin. And we remember the ancient wisdoms that always has been and always will be spiraling through our lives, linking one to another as thread woven through cloth; individuality within family, family within community, community within humanity, and finally humanity upon the earth. For we are made from the elements of the earth, and the earth is made from us. She is made from our ash and from our blood, and she in return remains our hearth.

As we treat ourselves with joy and compassion, so may we come to treat the earth. And as we treat the earth with joy and compassion, so may we learn to treat ourselves. Released then from the fear that has driven us into closets of inaction, released from the powerlessness that has paralyzed not only individual lives, but that has placed our increasingly fragile earth on the endangered species list, we will no longer have to reach out of ourselves to find Source or God. We will know God. We will not have to conquer other nations. We will live in peace with other nations. Making room for our life's breath and our life's spirit to enter into our bodies, we will re-orient ourselves in the flesh, on the earth in a global community. Then, perhaps, deep in our souls, deep in our skins we will find a joy and a peace that passes all understanding.

Walking the journey with simple steps that are erased in time,
We leave the paths clear and fresh with just the trees and hills behind.
That in its self is a life filled with Joy.
That in its self is one gift.

Thank you our reader for serving in this circling spiral dance.

CONTRIBUTORS

LISA ALVARADO is a poet, performance artist and dancer, and the author of several chapbooks of poetry, including *"The Housekeeper's Diary,"* her most ambitious work to date, based on her experiences as a maid for one of Chicago's wealthiest families. She has also adapted "The Housekeeper's Diary" into a one-woman performance with successful runs in Washington D.C. and Chicago. Lisa has been interviewed extensively by local and national media, including National Public Radio (Latino USA). She is currently writing a bisexually-themed book of erotica, "Erotica/Heroica", scheduled for release in 2004. She believes in the word made flesh and the flesh in the word.

SUSAN D. ANDERSON, wearied from a long career in education, took off for a two-year solitude in a house on a tiny island off the coast of Maine, and proclaimed herself a writer. Living the writing life at the edge of that wilderness provided her with uncountable moments of healing, rejoicing, and ripening from within. Anderson is currently working as a quality assurance analyst for a research company. She plans to return to the writing life when she retires.

MYRTLE ARCHER spent her childhood in the remoteness of northern Idaho, before moving to the San Francisco area. Her Civil War novel, *The Young Boys Gone,* was published by Walker and Co., NY, and is also in print in Canada and Germany. She is a consultant on creative writing projects and has taught "Writing for Publication." She is married to Howard Spracklen and they have a son, Jay.

LINDA ASHEAR served for five years as Managing Editor of *The Croton Review.* She has published two collections of poetry, *Toward the Light* and *The Rowers, The Swim-mers and the Drowned.* She has served as a preliminary judge for the annual Greenburgh poetry contest. Her poems have appeared in many anthologies and literary magazines, including *The Santa Barbara Review, Without Halos, The Laurel Review,* and *Light.* She runs writing workshops with school children, adult continuing education students, senior citizens, and people with AIDS, and teaches poetry writing one-on-one to private students. She loves doing poetry readings.

LOIS BARTH is an actress, writer, singer, storyteller who has developed three one-person shows in New York City and San Francisco. She is an original member of We Tell Stories, a touring storytelling company committed to promoting self-esteem in children through the use of literature. Her new solos piece, *"Reflections of an Urban Goddess"* was performed at the Actor's Theatre Workshop in NYC, 1996, and she is the recipient of a Poet and Writers grant.

KATE BARNES is the daughter of writers Elizabeth Coatsworth and Henry Beston. She lives on a farm in Maine that raises hay and blueberries. Her most recent book of poetry, *Where the Deer Were*, Godine 1994, has just come out in a paperback edition. Her poems have appeared in *American Scholar, The New Yorker, Village Voice,* and many other periodicals.

ELLEN BLAIS retired in December 2001 from the Department of Languages and Literature at Mansfield University in Mansfield, PA. where she has taught literature and composition for the past thirty years. She plans to do lots of writing in retirement. Two of her essays, *Consider the Snake* and *Huntress No More*, were published in the nature-writing journal Snowy Egret. The editors submitted "Consider the Snake" for consideration to the editors of the 2000 edition of *Pushcart Prize*.

LYN BLEILER is a freelance writer and published poet. Her poems have appeared in literary publications such as The California State Poetry Quarterly and Nimrod International Journal. She received an honorary mention in the New Jersey Theatre Guild's Poetry Competition. Lyn lives in Taos, New Mexico.

SUSAN CAMERON is the author of nine plays, all produced in NYC and in Los Angeles. Her recently published play, *"Flights,"* was a winner of the 2002 Samuel French Playwriting Competition. Production companies have optioned two of her five screenplays, and she wrote, directed, and starred in the short film "Reasonable Doubt" which was picked for the Philadelphia Film Festival. As an actress, Susan performed Off-Broadway in regional theater, as well as on ABC-TV's daytime drama "Loving," and in leading roles in several independent films. Susan is also a speech and dialects instructor, and has taught at Circle In the Square Theatre School and The Lee Strasburg Theater Institute. She currently teaches in the MFA program at The Actor's Studio and at New York University. She holds an MFA in acting from The Yale School of Drama.

JANINE CANAN, a Sonoma CA psychiatrist, has authored 13 collections of poetry, most recently *In the Palace of Creation: Selected Works 1969–1999*, and *Changing Woman*. She edited the acclaimed anthology, *She Rises like the Sun: Invocations of the Goddess;* translated German Jewish poet Else Lasker-Schüler in *Star in My Forehead;* edited the last work of avant-garde poet Lynn Lonidier in *The Rhyme of the Ag-ed Mariness;* and has edited *In the Language of the Heart: Messages from Amma*, a living saint. Janine's stories, *Journeys with Justine*, illustrated by Cristina Biaggi, will soon be out. She is poetry editor for *Awakened Woman* online. You may visit her at JanineCanan.com.

PHYLLIS CAPELLO, Brooklyn's own Ukulele Lady, is a writer/musician. She teaches poetry with Teachers & Writers Collaborative, gives family concerts, and entertains hospitalized children with The Big Apple Circus Clown Care Unit. She's a New York Foun-dation for the Arts fellow in fiction and a winner in the Allen Ginsberg Poetry Awards. Her work appears in many anthologies.

SHARON CHARDE, a psychotherapist in Lakeville, Ct, has led writing workshops and weekend retreats for women in Lakeville, CT. and Block Island, Rhode Island, since 1992. She won Honorable Mention in contests sponsored by *Maryland Poetry Review* and the Hannah Kahn Poetry Foundation, and has been finalist in the 2001 *Comstock Review,* 2003 Bordighera Poetry Prize and the 2003 Sunken Garden contest. She has been published in *Calyx,* the *Homestead Review,* and two anthologies, and has edited an antho-logy of poetry, *I Am Not A Juvenile Delinquent.* She is a grandmother and mother to two sons and has lived in Lakeville, CT. for thirty two years with her husband John.

EDITH CHEITMAN/SAIYNAMA is a crone dwelling in Maine. She has formerly been employed as a psychotherapist, market researcher, bartender, professor of social work, ice cream truck driver, encyclopedia sales person and tarot consultant, not necessarily in that order. She is currently devoting most of her time to looking out her window and re-Membering the Mother God. She makes very good corn chowder but prefers to go out for lunch—just in case you're in the area. Oh, yes, she's published poetry in innumerable small press magazines.

VIVINA CIOLLI's poems have received numerous prizes including First Place for her poem, *Photograph* judged by William Stafford. *Bitter Larder* won the 1994 New Spirit Press Poetry Chapbook Competition, and *Consolation of Dreams* was a 2001 winner of the Talent House Press Poetry Chapbook Competition. As a Fellow, she has furthered her work at Virginia Center for the Creative Arts, Dorset Colony House, Birdcliffe Arts Colony, The Ragdale Foundation and Villa Montalvo Center for the Arts. Ms. Ciolli is now working on a full-length collection of poems inspired by letters her husband wrote in the late 60's while stationed in Viet Nam. She is also working on a book of essays inspired by her cats: Fuzzy, Boozy, Mo Mo and Choo Choo. She holds degrees from St. Joseph's College, Queens College, and CCNY.

JUDITH BETH COHEN's novel *Seasons* was published by *The Permanent Press of Sag Harbor,* New York, 1984. Her work has appeared in *The North American Review, High Plains Literary Review, Rosebud, Sojourner, The Christian Science Monitor,* and *The Women's Review of Books.* She is the recipient of numerous grants and fellowships. She won a Pen Syndicated Fiction Award and was a Fullbright scholar in 1987. She has taught at Harvard University, Goddard College, Lesley College and Bard College.

MARY CRESCENZO's poetry, fiction and creative nonfiction have been included in anthologies by *Crossing Press, Milkweed Editions, Pig Iron Press, mala femmina press,* and in numerous literary journals. Her nonfiction and essays focusing on film, travel, arts and lifestyle, have appeared in *Cosmopolitan, The Writer, Playboy, The Santa Fe Repor-ter* and *The New Mexican.* Her radio broadcasting work began on WPLJ/ABC-FM, New York, as "Mary the Exercise Lady" with a morning drive exercise and nutrition feature, in the mid 1970's. Besides being a writer and broadcaster, she is a poetry performance and installation artist focusing on community issues.

ELIZABETH CUNNINGHAM is a novelist and poet. Her most recent works are *Small Bird: Poems & Prayers* and *Daughter of the Shining Isles,* Volume 1 of the *Magdalen Trilogy.*

R. H. DOUGLAS, born in Trinidad and Tobago, is a poet, performance artist and keeper of diaries for over 25 years. She is the co-founder of *SpiritWoman,* a writing and performing trio, that successively choreographed the poem, *Myth, Madness, Magic* at the Harold Clurman and Samuel Beckett Theatres. Her published works include *Erotique Noire/Black Erotica,* Doubleday 1992, *Lifenotes,* (Personal Writings by Contemporary Black Women,) W.W. Norton '94, and *Patchwork of Dreams, Creation Fire,* and *Pearls of Passion.*

ALTHA EDGREN is a wannabe novelist, medical writer, and mother of a Stony Brook-bound daughter and a blue-haired, black-clothed son. Outnumbered by cats, she lives in Stillwater, Minnesota with just slightly more flowers than weeds in her garden. She has several published poems to her credit and is in the midst of writing six different novels.

TAMARA ENGEL likes wearing different hats. She is an individual and family therapist, teacher of Insight Meditation, collage artist and writer. She is co-author of *Treating The Remarried Family* (Brunner/Mazel). Her essay on Lundy's Restaurant appears in *The Brooklyn Cookbook* Knopf). She recently moved from New York City to Florida to devote herself to the memoir in haiku and prose that she and her mother are writing about their relationship and how shopping has shaped it.

ALICE FRIMAN's latest book, *Zoo,* University of Arkansas Press, 1999, won the Ezra Pound Poetry Award from Truman State University. She is the recipient of an Indiana Arts Commission Fellowship, 1996–1997, and a Creative Renewal Fellowship 1999–2000 from the Arts Council of Indianapolis. She has been named to the 2002–2002 Georgia Poetry Circuit. She is the winner of many prizes and has been published in twelve countries.

HELEN FROST is the author of *Keesha's House* (Farrar, Straus & Giroux, 2003, Frances Foster Books), *When I Whisper, Nobody Listens: Helping Young People Write About Difficult Issues* (Heinemann, 2001), and *Skin of a Fish, Bones of a Bird* (Ampersand, 1993). She lives in Fort Wayne, Indiana, where she teaches poetry in schools, group homes, and juvenile detention facilities.

FRANCESCA GARVEY is a writer who has won several awards for her work, including the Young Georgia Playwrights for *Ce Mac Mathair*, and the Allan Bennett for *The Tragedy of Alba-Eire-Africa in America*. She has one unpublished novel, *Craifecht*, and several short published pieces to her credit. In addition, she has published numerous academic pieces and holds a MA in Renaissance Culture from the University of Sussex. She is currently completing her Ph.D. at Sussex and hopes to publish a dissertation about her research into English crime fiction.

MARILYN A. GELMAN's essays and light verse about growing up in Paterson, New Jersey, suburban single parenthood, commuting on the railroad, and living with trauma-tic brain injury (TBI) have appeared in The New York Times, in New Jersey newspapers, in national and literary magazines, and on radio.

WENDY GOULSTON has taught college literature, writing and interdisciplinary courses since 1969 in Australia, Israel, and the United States, for the last fourteen years at Empire State College, State University of New York. She writes poetry, memoirs and scholarly articles. She studies and practices movement meditation ("authentic movement"). She now lives with her husband and two children in New Rochelle, New York.

MELANIE HAMMER's fiction and essays have appeared in numerous magazines, including *The Ohio Review, The Nebraska Review, descant, Under the Sun,* and *The Missouri Review*. She lives in Astoria, New York, and teaches writing at Nassau Community College.

MARY DIANE HAUSMAN was born and raised in the Texas Hill Country, and now resides on the East Coast. Her writing is the voice of her healing, history and spirit. Her work appears in *Unsilenced: The Spirit of Women;* her own poetry collection, *A Born-Again Wife's First Lesbian Kiss,* and numerous other anthologies and literary journals. She holds a B.A. in Creative Writing from Empire State College (SUNY) where she also taught poetry and writing workshops. She will be ordained in 2003 as an Interfaith minister. She continues to integrate Spirit and Goddess energy with her writing and living.

KAREN HENNINGER grew up in a Pennsylvania Dutch farm family of nine. Domestic chores and child care were a large part of life. In 1995 she received a BFA/Related Arts, Major in Visual Arts, minors in English and Women Studies. She had her first art show, Stories of My Mothers, which included paintings, drawings and a booklet of prose, poetry and short stories. One of her paintings titled *Invisible Work* was part of the video installation at the United Nations Fourth World Conference on Women in Beijing, China. She has created a seminar series titled Women's Histories, Women's Realities and You. She has had articles, poems and short stories published and won two awards for her short stories. Her work continues to speak out in concern for women's issues.

PAT HENNON is a retired social worker. She remains active in community service as a board member on two Northwest Arkansas land trust projects. Also, she is on a board in the city of Fayetteville which provides low to moderate income housing in it's target area. "My strong commitment to community, nature and creativity is a healing commitment. I live in the woods and do creative work daily because I have to keep my healing process moving along. I am also known as Path Walker."

LARAINE HERRING is an author, teacher, creative counselor, and certified Grief-Recovery Specialist. She received her MFA from Antioch University and currently teaches creative writing at Phoenix Community College. She has also developed numerous workshops, which use writing as a tool for healing through grief and loss. *Duality Press* published her first book of prose and poetry, *Monsoons*, in 1999. She is also a playwright and editor, and her work has been widely anthologized. Her novel, *Lay my Sorrows Down*, won the Barbara Deming Award for Women in December, 2000. She has just completed a novel and is working on a non-fiction book about using writing as a tool for recovery through loss and transition.

ALLEGRA HOWARD is earning her master's degree in English and American literature, with a minor in creative writing from Harvard University. Her poetry and prose have appeared in *Turnstile, The Writing Self, Modern Haiku, Mayfly, Paragraph,* and *black bough*. She is currently completing her memoir, *Representative Woman*. She has a son who is 17 years old.

PAT HUYETT has taught English at the University of Missouri, Kansas City, since 1982. Her work has appeared in *Pleiades, Uncle, Webster Review, Poet & Critic, New Letters, Midway Review, Any Key Review, Recursive Angel, New Laurel Review, Sing, Heavenly Muse!, Yellow Silk* and *Main Street Poetry Journal.* "Girlfriends" is from the chapbook *Eldorado Rosa: Voices from Midtown* and is based on a true story of abortion before Roe vs. Wade.

RUTH INNES grew up in Pennsylvania, joined the Foreign Services, lived in many parts of the world and finally settled down in Jensen Beach, Florida. She has sold stories, poems and articles to such publications as *Mature Living, Hollins Critic, The Gem, Art Times, Word of Mouth – Vol 1, Sexual Harassment – Women Speak Out.* Many of her stories and poems have been published in small/literary magazines.

HESTIA IRONS is a survivor of childhood sexual abuse, spousal abuse, and drug and alcohol addiction. She has put her life together through Goddess Spirituality, and reaches out to help other "wounded" sisters by sharing her story and saying, "I know. I know your pain." She writes: "Yes, there is hope. I am 49, and it is never too late to heal."

JOY JONES is a speaker, storyteller and the author of several books: *Between Black Women: Listening With The Third Ear,* the acclaimed children's, *Tambourine Moon,* and *Private Lessons: A Book of Meditations for Teachers.* Her plays have been seen on stages in California, New York and Washington, D.C. *Outdoor Recess* won the Promising Playwrights Award, from Colonial Players of Annapolis, Md. in 1997. She is director of The Spoken Word Performance Poetry Ensemble.

EVELYN KELLMAN has been published in *Writing For Our Lives, Perceptions, Poet's Pen, S.L.U.G, San Diego Union Tribune, L.A. Times, Houston Post, Unitarian Universalist Poets – A Contemporary Survey* (1996) and elsewhere. She has won numerous poetry awards, and is currently working on the "What Shall We Tell Molly Project," a volume of mature women's wisdom for survival in a still patriarchal time. She prays nightly for a perfect world where all writers have secretaries and all gifts are postage stamps.

PATRICIA KELLY has been writing since her teens, and has been involved in the New York City poetry scene for over 25 years. Her poetry has won first place prizes from The Feminist Writers Guild and The New York Open Center Goddess Festival. She has taught creative writing at locations like The Manhattan Lighthouse for the Blind and the Brooklyn Public Library Children's Room. Patricia's website, "Pegasus Dreaming" (www.suite101.com/myhome.cfm/PegasusDreaming) explores dreams, poetry and Tarot, the heart of which is a collection by various authors of dream and Tarot-based creative writing unique on the web.

CYNTHIA LA FERLE is a nationally published essayist and award-winning newspaper columnist based in Royal Oak, Michigan. Her work has been published in *The Christian Science Monitor, Reader's Digest, Writer's Digest, Mary Engelbreit's home Companion, Unity Magazine,* and many others. She is author of an essay collection, *Old Houses, Good Neighbors* (Self-Reliance Press) and writes Haiku in her spare time.

HELENE LeBLANC is the author of *From the Grape to the Glass,* a wine and food book, which has sold over 10,000 copies, and a novel, *Summer Boy.* She lives on a working vineyard, and works as a freelance writer and wine educator. Her short stories, published in Adams Media Corporation, will be released in the Fall of 2001. She has had fiction and essays published in *International Living, The Liguorian, Napa Valley Register, St. Anthony's Messenger, True Story* and *Napa Valley Magazine.*

RUTH LEHRER retired from teaching elementary school 19 years ago at the age of 56. She began writing personal essays a few years later, after a bad medical experience that needed to be exorcised, and continues freelance writing in this venue. "It's the best therapy around," she declares. Ruth, along with her husband Arthur, is an Elderhostel coordinator in the Catskills, and enjoys the marvels of the Big Apple.

LYN LIFSHIN's most recent prizewinning book, (Paterson poetry award) *Before It's Light,* published winter 1999–2000 by Black Sparrow press, following their publication of *Cold Comfort* in 1997, reprinted in 2001. Black Sparrow continues to publish a series of her books including *Blue Sheets* in 2002. She has published more than 100 books of poetry, including *Marilyn Monroe, Blue Tattoo,* won awards for non-fiction, and edited four anthologies of women's writing including *Tangled Vines, Ariadne's Thread, and Lips Unsealed.* Her poems have appeared in most literary and poetry magazines, and she is the subject of an award winning documentary film, *Lyn Lifshin: Not Made of Glass,* available from Women Make Movies. Her web site is www.lynlifshin.

ROSEANN LLOYD's next book, *Because of the Light,* will be published by Holy Cow! Press, Fall, 2003. Other books include *War Baby Express,* Holy Cow! Press, 1996, *Tap Dancing for Big Mom,* New Rivers Press, 1986, and *JourneyNotes: Writing for Recovery and Spiritual Growth,* co-authored with Rochard Solly. She co-edited, with Deborah Keenan, *Looking for Home: Women Writing about Exile* (Milkweed Editions) which received an American Book Award from the Before Columbus Foundation, 1991. You can read some of the poems on her website at: www.CyberPoet.com/RoseannLloyd.html. Lloyd was born in Springfield, Missouri, and currently lives and works in Minneapolis, Minnesota.

KARA MANNING's plays have been produced, read or workshopped at London's Royal Court Theatre, MCC Theater, The Directors' Company, Makor, Ensemble Studio Theatre, Expanded Arts, Theatre for the New City, Bloomington Playwrights Project, and more. She is a recipient of the 2000-2001 Jerome Foundation, Affiliated Writers Program grant and is a member of the MCC Theater Playwrights' Coalition and the Dramatists' Guild. She was a resident playwright at The Royal Court's Playwrights/ Directors International Workshop and was an assistant director at

Edinburgh's Traverse Theatre during the 1997 Fringe Festival. She has written for *Rolling Stone*, MTV News and wrote liner notes for the Grammy-nominated Rhino box set "Respect: A Century of Women in Music." She is a 1998 graduate of Columbia University's M.F.A. program in playwriting.

JOAN MCMILLAN is a student in the MFA program at San Jose State University. She has published poems in numerous literary magazines and anthologies, including in *Poetry*, ONTHEBUS, *Quarry West*, and *Maryland Poetry Review*. In May of 2001, she was the recipient of the Mary Lonnberg Smith Poetry Award from Cabrillo College. She lives in Santa Cruz County, California, and is the mother of four marvelous children.

JANELL MOON is the author of four books of poetry including *The Mouth of Home*, published by Arctos Press. *Stirring the Waters: Writing to Find Your Spirit*, (Charles E. Tuttle) came out in May 2001, and Weiser Press published her second nonfiction, *The Wise Earth Answers*, in 2002. She teaches at the community college in Marin and San Francisco and has a private practice as a hypnotherapist and counselor at San Francisco City College.

KATHLEEN M. MOORE writes, "My writing always involves other people who have been important in my life. My published works are about my son *"Single Mother, Single Son"* in *A Single Mother's Companion*: an elderly woman friend *"Mama"* in *26 Minnesota Writers*: my Ethiopian students, *"Returning" in An Inn Near Kyoto*. Now I'm helping refugee women to write their own stories."

LAURA ROGERSON MOORE teaches English at Lawrence Academy in Groton, Massachusetts, where she lives with her husband and three daughters. She has had short fiction and poetry published in various journals and magazines, and is currently at work on a full-length manuscript.

MARY MURPHY is a writer and teller of stories. She has performed one-woman shows at several national conferences. Her stories have been anthologized in *Give A Listen: Stories of Storytelling in Schools* (NCTE, 1994) and *The Solstice Evergreen: The History, Folklore and Origins of the Christmas Tree*, (Aslan Press, 1998) and published in such periodicals as *Sacred Journey* and *The Artful Mind*. Her website is at http://www.albany. net/~hello/.

MARIKO NAGAI's poems are stories have appeared in *Asian Pacific American Journal*, *The Gettysburg Review*, *New Letters*, *Prairie Schooner*, *Southern Review*, and other journals. She received the Pushcart Prizes both in poetry (1998) and fiction (2001). Graduate of the New York University Master's program in Creative Writing (poetry) where she was the Remarque fellow, she has received fellowships and scholarships from Writer's Con-ferences and Festivals, Mount Holyoke Writer's Conference, Catskill Poetry Workshop, Breadloaf Writer's Conference, and Vermont Studio Center, and writing residency fellowships from Hedgebrook Foundation (August 2002), and Art Omi/Ledig House (April–May 2003). Currently, she teaches Japanese literature and creative writing at Temple University Japan in Tokyo, Japan, where she is also the Acting Director of the Writing Programs and Freshman Writing Program.

DORRIT ANDERSON O'LEARY probably began writing poetry as soon as she began to write. A child of Swedish immigrants from Värmland who settled in Massachusetts, she had a long career as an advertising executive with her husband and later as a poetry teacher in Newton, MA. She received an NEH grant to complete a book of poems, *Scrambling the Stones*, which was published after her death in 1986.

STEPHANIE PALL published three contemporary romance novels, (writing as Stephanie Kincaid), and translated books into braille. She spent most of her adult life in Maine, a state she loved for its beauty, its remoteness and its iconoclasm. She was an accomplished flutist, and toward the end of her life, she adopted the practice of Buddhism. Ill health plagued her and she died in 1988 at the age of 45, leaving behind more than 800 carefully worked poems.

NITA PENFOLD is a writer, artist, and educator in the New England area. Over 350 of her poems and several short stories have been published in the past 20 years. Pudding House Publications published a chapbook of her poetry, *The Woman With the Wild-Grown Hair* in 1998, and *Mile-High Blue-Sky Pie* in 2002. Her work has appeared in the anthologies: *Cries of the Spirit, Catholic Girls, Claiming the Spirit Within,* and *Sacred Voices: 4000 Years of Women's Wisdom.*

ELISAVIETTA RITCHIE's books include *In Haste I Write You This Note: Stories & Half-Stories and Raking the Snow* (both winners, Washington Writers' Publishing House awards); *Flying Time: Stories & Half-Stories* (4 PEN Syndicated Fiction winners); *Arc of the Storm; Elegy for the Other Woman: Tightening The Circle Over Eel County* (won Great Lakes Colleges Association's "New Writer's Award"). New manuscript, *Awaiting Permission to Land* won Anamnesis Poetry Award.

BARBARA A. ROUILLARD is a teacher and writer from Springfield, Massachusetts. Her poetry and short stories have appeared in over eighty-five publications and anthologies, including *Yankee, Amelia, Midwest Poetry Review, Happy, Feminist Voices, Writer's Journal, ByLine, Poetry in Motion,* and *Verve.* In 1994, Ms. Rouillard received a NEH Fellowship, and she is a recipient of a Massachusetts Cultural Council

Professional Development Grant. She also won first prize in the 1996 Allen Ginsberg Poetry Awards, Poetry Center, Passaic County Community College. Barbara recently completed a book of creative nonfiction entitled *Whosoever Brings Them Up*. She has a twenty-six year old daughter.

JOANNA C. SCOTT is the author of *Indochina's Refugees: Oral Histories from Loas, Cambodia and Vietnam; Charlie and the children*, a novel of Vietnam (VVA Veteran Book-of-the-Month); and *The Lucky Gourd Shop*, a novel of Korea (Book Sense Top Ten Titles pick). *Birth Mother*, poetry of adoption, won the Longleaf Press Poetry Award, *Coming Down from Bataan*, poetry of the Philippines, the Acorn-Rukeyser Award, and *New Jerusalem* the Capricorn Poetry Award. Ms. Scott lives in Chapel Hill, North Carolina.

SUSANNE SENER is a part-time teacher and full-time writer and editor, having published many technical and business articles, manuals, reports, and corporate newsletters. Her personal essays on women's issues have appeared or are forthcoming in *Woman's World Weekly, Walking*, and *Threads*. She lives on the top of a mountain in Colorado, along with three dogs, two old sewing machines, a wood-burning stove, and plenty of wood to chop! She dieted and exercised compulsively from age 13 to 30, until she moved to the mountain and realized that good health resulting from moderate exercise and life-sustaining food is far more important than the numbers on a scale or a pair of jeans.

DEBORAH SHOUSE is a creativity coach, editor, teacher and dreamer. Her work has appeared in *Ms., Woman's Day, Family Circle, Hemispheres* and *Reader's Digest, News-week, Redbook, Christian Science Monitor*, and *The Sun*. Deborah is also the author of a number of business books, the co-author of *Antiquing for Dummies*, and the creator of a CD, *Everyday Heroes*, a collection of her stories. Deborah is the mother of two intense intelligent daughters. She dreams of finding the right words and making a difference. Her website is www.thecreativityconnection.com

ELAINE STARKMAN is the author of *Learning to Sit in the Silence: A Journal of Caretaking, Elderbooks*, and editor of *Here I Am: Contemporary Jewish Stories from Around the World*, which won the PEN/Oakland Award. Her poem "Okay in Berkeley" was published in *Moving: Poems: 1992–2002* and is available at estarkma@dvc.edu. She lives in the East Bay in Northern California.

BEVERLY TRICCO enjoys encapsulating herself into brief bios. She writes to bring what's inside... out. Some of her work has been published in anthologies, quarterlies and magazines like *Prayers To Protest, Light Me Through, The Aurorean, The Café Review, Curmudgeon, Earth's Daughters, Epiphanies in P major, The New Times*,

SageWoman, Spirit of Change and *Poor Katy's Almanac.* She is the Director of Religious Education at Unity Church in North Easton, MA. In addition to that job, she has a family and pets and friends and refuels to simplify her life. She likes to tell herself she can juggle real life and magic.

B. LOIS WADAS is a Director, Playwright, Poet and Performance Artist based in NYC. She twice moderated "A Round Table of Women Writers," aired on Manhattan Network Television in NYC. Lois is an active member of The International Women Writers Guild, and a member of the Dramatist Guild. Lois directed Ntozake Shanges *For Colored Who Have Considered Suicide When The Rainbow is Enuf* at SUNY Stony Brook. She recently Produced and Directed her play *Woman to Woman* at the Harlem Theatre Co. in NYC. Lois appeared on HBO in the *Vagina Monologues.* As a Psychotherapist, Lois firmly believes "an unexamined life is a life unlived."

JOEY WAUTERS retired from chairing the English Department at the University of Alaska Southeast in Juneau. Her literary honors include first place in *Redbook's* Short Story Contest, and poetry awards in contests sponsored by *Writer's Digest,* The National League of American Pen Women, and the American Chapbook Awards. She has published poetry and fiction in *Zone 3, Hudson Valley Echoes, Sow's Ear Poetry Review,* and *Poet Magazine* among others. Recent publication in fiction and creative nonfiction appear in *Dominican Review* and *An Ear to the Ground.*

COLLEEN M. WEBSTER was born in Sunnyvale, California on the last day of summer, and grew up outside of Washington, D.C. where she received her Bachelor's degree in English from the College of Notre Dame of Maryland. For the past nine years she has given local readings and published works in local and national journals. Currently she is researching and writing her doctoral dissertation on the poetry of Rukeyser, Rich, Piercy, Olds and Walker, teaching full time for Harford Community College and coaching on the college level.

GRATEFUL ACKNOWLEDGMENTS

ulimia" by Lisa Alvarado, appeared in her Chapbook, *Reclamo*. "Inside-Out" by Linda Ashear, appeared in *Embers*, 1993. "Dear Body" by Janine Canan is from *Her Magnificent Body: New & Selected Poems*, by Janine Canan, copyright 1986, Janine Canan, published by Manroot Press. "Demeter's Undoing" by Phyllis Capello has appeared in *Footwork: The Paterson Review*, 1996 & VIA: *Voices in Italian Americana-Special Issue on Italian American Women Authors*, 1997. "Hysterectomy," by Sharon Charde, first appeared in *The Women's Times*, a regional publication for women in and around the Berkshires of Western Massachusetts, in their May/June 1994 issue, copyright 1994. Reprinted with permission of The Women's Times. "Taking Off and Landing – A New Narrative," by Judith Beth Cohen, copyright 1995, appeared in *Changes, The Recovery Lifestyle Magazine*. Another version appeared in *Writing For Our Lives*, Vol. 4, #2, 1996, publisher Running Deer Press, Los Gatos, California. "To My Mother, " by Elizabeth Cunningham, was first published in the December 1991 issue of *Radcliffe Quarterly*. "The Good News," by Alice Friman, first appeared in *The Cream City Review*, Vol. 18 no. 1, Spring 1984, and reprinted in her book, *Inverted Fire*, BkMk Press, 1997. "Labor of Dreams" by Mary Diane Hausman first appeared in *A Born-Again Wife's First Lesbian Kiss and Other Poems*, by Mary Diane Hausman, copyright 1995, published by Relief Press, 1995. "Reflections from a Holy Place" by Mary Diane Hausman, copyright 1992 by Mary Diane Hausman, was first published in *Color Wheel 6*, by 700 Elves Press, 1992, Frederick Moe, publisher, and again in *A Born-Again Wife's First Lesbian Kiss and Other Poems*, Relief Press, 1995, and *Unsilenced: The Spirit of Women*, Commune-a-Key Press, 1997. "City Dweller" by Laraine Herring, first appeared in *Monsoons: A Collection of Writing*, by Laraine Herring, copyright 1999, Duality Press, Phoenix, AZ. "Coming of Age – Kansas City 1970," by Pat Huyett, first appeared in her chapbook, *Eldorado Rosa: Voices from Midtown*. "Dancing With Mom" by Joy Jones first appeared in *The Washington Post*, May 10, 1995. "We Really Have Come a Long Way" by Evelyn Kellman originally appeared in *The San Diego Union Tribune*, November 24, 1993. "Becoming a Writer," and "Crescent Moon," by Roseann Lloyd were originally published in *War Baby Express* by Roseann Lloyd, copyright 1996, Holy Cow! Press. "$25 an Hour at the

ABOUT ELIZABETH WELLES

Elizabeth Welles loves the art of storytelling in any form, and playing with the Word, be it on the stage or the page. She has worked in the corporate and theatrical worlds, and has traveled, performed, studied, and taught both in this country and abroad as writer, actor, and teacher.

As a wordsmith, she is the author of wacky and dramatic monologues, screenplays, articles, poetry and song, and the play *Speak the Lands of My Heart,* about one woman's cross-cultural journey into the heart of India. As an actor she performs her own works on the New York and LA stage, has been in television and film, and has done numerous readings in a variety of venues.

A Creative Intuitive, Elizabeth lectures and teaches on the creative process and *Journaling for Well-being and Peace.* She is the founder of *The ISIS Method for Stress Reduction;* its main premise being that when one is involved with what they love, stress is reduced. Adding joy and spice to a life, individuals the world over find inspiration and encouragement to explore their unique creativity. Private clients artfully move with the transitions in their lives to fulfill personal dreams and goals, while learning to trust their own intuitive voices.

Her company, *Peace Communications,* explores laughter, creativity and peace through the performing and literary arts. Additional information can be found on the web at www.PeaceCommunications.net.

If you'd like to sponsor a workshop or lecture on *Women Celebrate, Journaling for Well-being and Peace,* or on creativity and stress reduction, please write Elizabeth at 1129 Maricopa Highway #200, Ojai, CA 93023 or through the web.

ORDER FORM

Women Celebrate

Peace Communications
1129 Maricopa Highway #200
Ojai, CA 93023

Please send me _____ copies at $15.95 each.

California residents add 7.25% sales tax (at $1.16 each).

For media-rate shipping, add $3.50 for first book, and $0.75 for each additional book.

To expedite shipping or to place large orders please contact us on the web at www.PeaceCommunications.net.

Total enclosed: $_____

Ship books to: _____

_____

_____

Books can be ordered through any bookstore, amazon.com, barnesandnoble.com, and in the United Kingdom and parts of Europe.

Printed in the United States
1365500002B/85-336